IGNORANCE

IGNORANCE

On the Wider Implications
of Deficient Knowledge

NICHOLAS RESCHER

University of Pittsburgh Press

Published by the University of Pittsburgh Press, Pittsburgh, Pa., 15260

Copyright © 2009, University of Pittsburgh Press

Manufactured in the United States of America

Printed on acid-free paper

10 9 8 7 6 5 4 3 2 1

Library of Congress Cataloging-in-Publication Data

Rescher, Nicholas.
  Ignorance : on the wider implications of deficient knowledge / Nicholas
Rescher.
      p. cm.
  Includes bibliographical references and index.
  ISBN-13: 978-0-8229-6014-0 (pbk. : alk. paper)
  ISBN-10: 0-8229-6014-1 (pbk. : alk. paper)
 1. Ignorance (Theory of knowledge)   2. Knowledge, Theory of
3. Cognition.   I. Title.
  BD221.R47 2009
  121—dc22   2008052956

For Henry Kyburg
Dedicated Philosopher

CONTENTS

PREFACE

Ignorance, so we are told, is bliss. But that is very questionable. Were it so, the human condition would be far happier than it actually is. Yet if ignorance is not the key to happiness, is it perhaps the key to wisdom? Some have thought so. In Plato's dialogical *Apology,* the Delphic oracle held Socrates to be the wisest of men because he realized that he knew nothing. But perhaps the oracle was misquoted. Perhaps it actually praised Socrates not for claiming to know nothing but for not claiming to know what he actually did not.

There are many different types of ignorance, prominently including that of the stupidity of one who cannot learn and that of the foolishness of one who will not learn. Neither of these is at issue here. For our present concern is specifically with the sort of unavoidable ignorance that besets man notwithstanding his best efforts and intentions.

The present book is a synthesis that brings together the results of various earlier investigations to give a coherent overall picture of the ramifications and implications of human ignorance. For the limits of our own knowledge represent a theme to which I have given much attention over the years, and this book is a work of synthesis. It seeks to weave together the ideas developed in various special investigations into a comprehensive tapestry that affords a systematic picture of the overall situation.

Not withstanding its emphasis on the extent of our ignorance, this book is certainly no foray in scepticism. Quite the reverse! For to argue that knowledge has its limits is to hold that it has its domain as well. The sceptic has it that no secure knowledge of fact is available. And this is absurd—although this volume is not the place to set out the reason why.[2] The really problematic issue is one the sceptic simply avoids with his all-out denial of knowledge—namely, that of setting out the burden between what is knowable and what is not, exploring its placement and examining its rationale.

Issues of the limits of knowledge and the limits of science have preoccupied me for many years, and the present book provides a convenient occasion for bringing the various threats of these discussions together in a synoptic and systematic examination of ignorance, thus returning to some of the themes that my medieval namesake Nicholas of Cusa addressed in his classic, *On Learned Ignorance*. As this learned author emphasized, discussions about ignorance need not—should not—themselves betray ignorance.

Ignorance prevails insofar as there are actual facts that one does not know, significant questions that one cannot cogently answer. It is a matter of defeat in regard to knowledge and is, next to outright error, the most serious form of cognitive deficiency there is. There is no alchemy by which we can transmute mere ignorance into knowledge—or indeed even into probabilities. (If we do not know *what* word was written on a card, we can not even be sure *that* a word was written there.)

That which perhaps more than anything else betokens the importance of ignorance is that there is so much of it about. Realizing the limited extent of one's knowledge is the beginning of wisdom.

Indeed, Diogenes Laertius tells us that Socrates mentioned that the only thing he knew for a fact was the reality of his own ignorance.[3]

Ignorance exists because man is a being of limited intelligence and power. We humans are finite beings—small potatoes in nature's grand scheme of things. And as beings of limited capacity, we cannot manage to wrap our minds adequately around the world's vast manifold of complex and complexly interrelated realities. Accordingly, there is nothing incidental or fortuitous about our ignorance—it is something deep-rooted in the nature of things.

But just how does this ignorance manifest itself and how far does it extend? And what are its implications for the human condition in general and our own prospects for happiness and well-being in particular? These are the key issues to which the present deliberations will be addressed. For, perhaps surprisingly, ignorance is itself a fertile topic of knowledge.

I find that in my recent work I am caught up in a dilemma. For my overall effort seeks to articulate a systematic position, and by nature a system involves interconnections and overlaps through pervasive interlinkages. This feature inevitably contains repetitions and redundancies in exposition among various expository books. For the interests of self-sufficiency in one branch calls for overlapping redundancy with another. From the angle of the average reader, this poses no problem. After all, it would be inappropriate hubris to suppose that the reader of one book knows the relevant material already expounded in another. But the reviewer, ideally an expert in the field who knows the general lay of the land, may well chafe at re-exposure to something familiar and find such redundancies objectionable. I see no help for this and will accept such reviewer complaints with stoic resignation. The book, after all, is being written for its readers rather than its critics.

I am grateful to Estelle Burris for her competent work in preparing this material for print.

IGNORANCE

The Reach of
Ignorance

WHAT IGNORANCE IS ALL ABOUT

Cognitive ignorance is the lack of knowledge of fact. Error is a matter of commission. With error we have the facts wrong. Ignorance, by contrast, is a matter of omission: with ignorance we do not have the facts, period. By and large, error is thus worse than ignorance. As Thomas Jefferson wrote: "Ignorance is preferable to error; and he is less removed from the truth who believes nothing, than he who believes what is wrong."[1] In a way this is true enough. Ignorance leaves us without guidance, error sends us off in the wrong direction. And frequently we are better off staying put.

However, the reality of it is that ignorance ("error of omission") often leads to outright error ("errors of commission"). Of course, ignorance is not an all-or-nothing matter; it is only too often a thing of aspects and facets. "Given me a five-letter word for *visitor* beginning with G," asks the crossword-puzzle solver. Granted, he does not know the word. But he has narrowed things down quite a bit.

The clearest index of ignorance is the inability to answer meaningful questions in a way that manages to convince people—ourselves included. For if a question is indeed authentically meaningful, then it will have an answer, and if we are unable to resolve that question then we are through this very fact ignorant of what the answer is. The inability to identify the answer convincingly is the clearest possible indication that we do not know it.

Often we do not simply respond to ignorance by leaving a mere blank. We have a natural and perfectly reasonable inclination to fill in those gaps in the easiest, most natural, and sometimes even most attractive way. Who has not overtaken some stranger on the road and been disappointed by the visage on which Reality decided? Who has not been startled by the actual deeds that filled the gap left open by a political candidate's vacuous campaign? Jumping to conclusions over a chasm of ignorance is a natural human tendency from which few of us are exempt.

There are as many sorts of ignorance as there are sorts of things to be ignorant about. And so even as knowledge knows no bounds, so does ignorance. The price of ignorance in general is incapacity. The person who does not know where to find food cannot eat. The person who does not know the combination cannot open the lock. The person who does not know how to start the engine cannot drive the car. Even as knowledge is power, so ignorance is impotence. This is a key motivator for hoarding information and keeping secrets.

It is even difficult to obtain a taxonomy of ignorance. For the realm of ignorance is every bit as vast, complex, and many faceted as that of knowledge itself. Whatever someone can know, they can also be ignorant about—arguably exempting a handful of Cartesian exceptions, such as the fact that knowers are pretty much bound ex officio to realize that they themselves exist and can think.

Ignorance encompasses a vast and varied terrain. All sorts of information is simply not available. Many aspects of reality vanish without a trace—the array of yesterday's clouds, for example. And much about the thought life of others is inscrutable to us, unless they tell us—and do so honestly. (What was on Napoleon's mind on the long journey to St. Helena?) But while such things are difficult—perhaps even impossible—to find out about them is not in principle unknowable. (We could have photographed yesterday's clouds—though we didn't. Napoleon could have pounded out his mind into a journal— thought he didn't.) Nobody knows the day on which the last of the Neanderthals died or what Caesar had for breakfast on that fateful Ides of March. But it is in theory possible that the requisite information should come to light—there is nothing inherently unattainable about it. The issue of contingent ignorance—of what people are too lazy or too incompetent to find out about—does not hold much interest for cognitive theory. What matters from the theoretical point of view are those aspects of ignorance that betoken inherent limits to human knowledge.

The ignorance of people can only be compared in this, that, or the other respect. To amalgamate ignorance overall would involve comparing apples and oranges. There is no way to measure ignorance. Perhaps information can be measured textually by comparing the space that needs to be dedicated to its storage—the size of library holdings or the computer bits involved. But ignorance is immeasurable: we cannot know the lineaments of the unknown.

If we adopt the distinction between *substantive* knowledge about the factual matters of some domain and *metaknowledge* about our knowledge itself, then it is going to transpire that even in domains where (as per the sceptic's contention) substantive knowledge is not to be had. Nevertheless, the prospect of metaknowledge remains open and indeed is bound to be nonempty in view of what is, by hypothesis, the fact of our knowing substantive knowledge to be unavailable. And so, to acknowledge pervasive ignorance is not to endorse scepticism. After all, to claim to know that there is nothing that one knows is a paradox. On the other hand, the claim that there are some things that we do not know affords us as secure a piece of knowledge as there is.

It is important to heed the distinction between facts that nobody *does actually* know and facts that nobody *can possibly* know—between merely unknown facts and inherently unknowable ones.[2] Of some things we are (and must remain) ignorant because of the world's contingent arrangements. Of others our ignorance lies in conceptual structure of the situation with regard to the item at issue. The really interesting issue, accordingly, relates not to that which *is not* known to some or even to all of us. The examples one can offer of the former are too many, and of the latter too few. Instead, the really interesting question relates to that which cannot be known at all. From the theoretical point of view, this represents the most interesting form of ignorance.

One of the most obvious sources of ignorance is the sheer volume of available factual information. There is so much out there to be known that any given individual cannot ever begin to make more than an insignificant fraction of it. The vastness of any given person's ignorance is unfathomable. Isaac Newton wrote of himself as "a boy standing on the seashore . . . whilst the great ocean of truth lay all underscored before me." This holds in spades for the rest of us. And, ironically, the more one learns, the more vast one's scope of ignorance is destined to become.

But are there actually any unknowable truths—cases in which there indeed are actual facts of the matter of such a sort that no one can possibly get to know them?

IGNORANCE ABOUT OUR OWN IGNORANCE IS FUNDAMENTAL

The very idea of cognitive limits has a paradoxical air. It suggests that we claim knowledge about something outside knowledge. But (to hark back to Hegel), with respect to the realm of knowledge, we are not in a position to draw a line between what lies inside and what lies outside—seeing that, ex hypothesi, we have no cognitive access to the latter. One cannot contemplate the relative extent of knowledge or ignorance about reality except by basing it on some picture of reality that is already in hand—that is, unless one is prepared to take at face value the deliverances of existing knowledge.

Now one key consideration here is that while one can know indefinitely *that* one is ignorant of something—that there are facts one does not know—one cannot know specifically *what* it is that one is ignorant of—that is, what the facts at issue are. One of the most critical yet problematic areas of inquiry relates to knowledge regarding our own cognitive shortcomings. It is next to impossible to get a clear fix on our own ignorance, because in order to know that there is a certain fact that we do not know, we would have to know the item at issue to be a fact, and just this is, by hypothesis, something we do not know. "Being a fact I do not know" is a noninstantiable predicate as far as I am concerned. (You, of course, could proceed to instantiate it.) But "being a fact that *nobody* knows is flat out noninstantiable—so that we here have a typical vagrant predicate.

Actually, if there is always a fact which a given individual does not know then there will be a fact that nobody knows. For if F_1 is a fact that X_1 does not know, and F_2 is a fact that X_2 does not know, then there will be a fact, namely F_1-and-F_2, which neither X_1 nor X_2 manages to know. And this cognitive route to unknown facts will extend across the entire landscape of existing individuals. There will, accordingly, have to be unknowns—facts that are not known to anyone at all.

To be sure, all we claim to know is *that* there are such facts. But *what* they are is itself one of those matters of unknowability. Obviously we cannot give an illustrative example of an unknown fact, seeing that this requires knowing the item to be a fact, contrary to hypothesis.[3] One can, in principle, illustrate ignorance by adding questions no one can answer, but indicating the detail of facts that nobody knows is totally impracticable for us.

The actual situation is not that of a crossword puzzle—or of geographic exploration—where the size of the terra incognita can be somehow measured in advance of securing the details that are going to be filled in. We can form no sensible estimate of the imponderable domain of what can be known but is not. To be sure, we can manage to compare what one person or group knows with what some other person or group knows. But mapping the realm of what is knowable as such is something that inevitably reaches beyond our powers. And for this reason any questions about the cognitive completeness of our present knowledge are and will remain inexorably unresolvable.

That our knowledge is sufficient for our immediate purposes—specifically by enabling us to answer the questions we then and there have before us—is something that is in principle readily determinable. But that it is *theoretically* adequate to answer not just our present questions but those that will grow out of them in the future is something we can never manage to establish. For it is clear that the sensible management of ignorance is something that requires us to operate in the realm of practical considerations exactly because the knowledge required for theoretical adequacy on this subject is—by hypothesis—not at our disposal. We have no cogently rational alternative to proceed, here as elsewhere, subject to the basic pragmatic principle of having to accept the best that we can do as good enough.

It is accordingly needful to distinguish between contingent and necessary ignorance. The former is the result of the way in which things work in the world—time covers its tracks, the future does not foreshadow its doings, chaos precludes prediction, that sort of thing. By contrast, necessary ignorance relates to situations where claiming knowledge leads to self-introduction. "I know that I am ignorant to the fact that" or "*f* is a fact I will never come to realize" would be paradigm illustrations, there being truths of this format I cannot possibly come to realize.

SPECIFIC VERSUS INDEFINITE KNOWLEDGE AND IGNORANCE

In this connection it is instructive to note some relatively simple but nevertheless far-reaching considerations regarding the project of rational inquiry and the limits of knowledge. Let Kxp as usual abbreviate "*x* knows that *p*." And now note the contrast between the contentions:

"*x* knows that something has the property *F*": $Kx(\exists u)Fy$

and

"*x* knows of something that *it* has the property *F*": $(\exists y)KxFu$

The variant placement of the quantifier means that there is a crucial difference here, since in the second case, unlike the first, the knower in question is in a position specifically to identify the item at issue. Here in this second case our knower not merely knows generally and indefinitely that *something* has *F*, but knows concretely and specifically *what it is* that has *F*. The two cognitive situations are clearly very different. To know that someone is currently in the Library of Congress is one thing, and to know who is there is quite another.

And this has wider ramifications. For the reality of it is that there is a world of difference between saying, "I don't know whether *p* is a fact" and saying "*p* is a fact that I don't know." The former is unproblematic, but the latter just doesn't make sense.[4]

Correspondingly, we must recognize that there is a crucial difference between the indefinite "I know that there is some fact that I do not know" and the specific "Such and such is a fact of which I know that I do not know it." The first is unproblematic but the second not, seeing that to know of something that it is a fact I must know it as such so that what is at issue is effectively a contradiction in terms. I can know about my ignorance only vaguely and generally *(sub ratione generalitatis)* at the level of indefiniteness, but I cannot know it in concrete detail. I can meaningfully hold that two and two's being four is a *claim* (or a *purported* fact) that I do not know to be the case, but cannot meaningfully maintain that two and two's being four is an *actual* fact that I do not know to be the case. To maintain a fact as fact is to assert knowledge of it: in maintaining p as a fact one claims to know that p.

And this has wider ramifications. For the reality of it is that there is a world of difference between saying "I don't know whether p is a fact" and saying "p is a fact that I don't know." The former comes down to maintaining that I neither know that p nor that not-p. No problem there. However, the second statement, to the effect that p is a fact that one doesn't know to be so, comes down to maintaining both that p is true and that I do not know this. Such a claim is clearly self-contradictory.[5]

SOME PRIME SOURCES OF IGNORANCE

THE UNAVAILABLE FUTURE

Perhaps the clearest and most decisive impediment to knowledge are our *conceptual* limitations. It was not for lack of intelligence of brain power that Caesar could not have known that his sword contained tungsten, but the very idea was not as yet available, that tungsten just did not figure on the conceptual agenda of the time. We cannot gain cognitive access to a fact whose conceptualization outruns available resources. It is not that the facts at issue are unknowable as such; their cognitive inaccessibility is to those to whom the requisite conceptual mechanism are unavailable. Those facts whose conceptualization awaits the innovations of an as-yet unrealized fabric are inevitably unknowable by the individuals of the present.

THE STATISTICAL FOG

Consider the inauguration of public safety measures. A speed limit is set, a traffic light installed, an inoculation campaign developed. There is no question that many lives are saved. But whose? Many among us would not be here if these steps had not been taken. Yet who are they? We know there are some who were saved by the measure but there is no way of telling who they are: this is something that nobody knows or indeed can know.[6] There are bound to be individuals of whom it is true that their life was so saved, and consequently there is a fact of the matter here: "X's life was saved" will—and will have to be—true for certain values of X, for certain individuals. But there is no possible way for us ever to identify such an individual. The fact at issue is an inherently unknowable fact. It is hidden away undetectably in a statistical fog. We know some of the generalities of the matter, but cannot possibly come to grips with the specifics.

The circumstance reflects the crucial difference between the cognitively infinite $K(\exists x)Sx$ and the cognitively specific $(\exists x)KSx$. We know that many lives have been saved by certain preventive measures. But there is no one we know whose life was saved by these measures. The issue of what specific lives were saved represents a paradigmatic instance of an unknowable fact. It is something whose identity is hidden out of our cognitive sight in the statistical fog induced by the chaotic character of nature causality.

THE STOCHASTIC UNIVERSE OF CHANCE

A coin is to be tossed. We know full well that it will come up heads or tails. But we do—and can—have no idea as to which it will be. This too is a salient substance of inevitable ignorance. Here we deal with items that are hidden out of our sight by the stochastic character of natural causality. Thus given an atom of a heavy and unstable trans-uranic element we can predict *that* it will decay but not when. How long it will last is a matter of inevitable ignorance.

THE RAVAGES OF TIME

The world's causal processes so unfold as to erase all traces of various realities that have been. The sand dunes of the past leave no detect-able traces in the desert of the present. The writing on the page is lost irretrievably when the paper is burned and its ashes scattered. The swans of yesteryear are undetectable in the waters of the present. And so even as much of the future is as-yet invisible, so much of the past has become as-of-now unvisited.

THE WAYS OF THE WORLD

The examples of unknowability that we have been considering—those rooted in undetectability, unpredictability, and irrecoverabil-ity—are all in their way inevitable given the nomic structure of natu-ral process. Each of them hinges on how things work in the world. They are necessary but *physically* necessary. In this regard, they stand in contrast with our ignorance regarding matters that we could read-ily find out about.

CULPABLE AND VINCIBLE IGNORANCE

Does ignorance have an ethical or moral dimension? Is it something blameworthy, or are the ignorant more to be practical than cen-sured? It all depends. For there is culpable ignorance and excusable ignorance. Excusable ignorance prevails in circumstances where there is a plausible excuse of the individual's being ignorant—an ex-cuse that renders it "only natural" that someone might be ignorant in the circumstances. Culpable ignorance, by contrast, is inexcusable— ignorance where we have every right and reason to expect that there should not be any. But ignorance about the extent of our own ignorance is for the most part excusable on grounds of inevitability. One surely cannot be blamed for a failure to know things that someone had not the opportunity to learn. (It would be absurd to reproach the travel agent of having booked passengers on the Titanic.) On the contrary!

Is ignorance as such a sin? Yes and no. Sometimes, to be sure, breaches of ignorance are problematic. There are, after all, things one ought not to know—other people's personal secrets, for example. Certain kinds of confidential or proprietary information belong to others. Lifting the veil of ignorance from information that, properly speaking, should be concealed can be inappropriate. There are certainly no general obligations to accumulate information at large and unrestrictedly. On the other hand, there is a body of information—generally characterized as "common sense"—which everyone is expected to know (for example, that long-term immersion in water causes people to drown). Additionally, there are categories of information that people are expected to know ex officio in virtue of their role or status as parents, as physicians, as algebra teachers, or whatever.

Culpable ignorance obtains when the requisite information is available, but insufficient, incompetent, or inadequate efforts are made to obtain it. While this sort of thing is perhaps the most frequent and widespread sort of ignorance, it is nevertheless of less theoretical interest than its contrary—venial or excusable ignorance. For the latter obtains in all of those situations where ignorance is inevitable because the requisite information regarding the fact is unavailable thanks to the general principles of the situation. It is this business of in-principle unattainable information that is at center stage throughout this volume.

Ignorance deserves censure only when it is culpably willful. Venial ignorance is in general remediable by adequate effort. Then, as the saying has it, "You can fix ignorance" (though it shrewdly goes on to say, "but you can't fix stupidity"). But often as not, ignorance is a perfectly appropriate defense against reproach: he simply had no way of knowing. Clearly, it would only be those cases in which culpable ignorance leads to untoward consequences where moral reproach would be in order.

One of the great defects of cognitive scepticism is that it annihilates the very idea of culpable ignorance. For if (per impossible) the sceptic were right and we could know nothing whatsoever, then of course ignorance of any and all sorts would be at once eventualities. Where no one can know anything, no one is open to reproach for a lack of knowledge.

That certain sorts of knowledge can be expected of, and must be at least provisionally attributed to, variously situated people is simply a matter of social common sense.

To be sure, besides informative ignorance there is also practical or performative ignorance: lack of know-how rather than lack of know-what. Even the best informed among us may well not know how to steer a supertanker or how to shear a sheep. And those sorts of possible ignorance will of course be culpable in a person who is supposed to know in virtue of his office or position.

Then, too, there is the distinction between vincible and invincible ignorance. Vincible ignorance is that which an individual can overcome with a reasonable amount of effort. Invariable ignorance, by contrast, can be overcome only with a substantial effort, if at all. If something significant is at stake—either *prudentially* in affecting a person's well-being or *morally* in affecting the well-being of others—we would expect people to devote duly proportionate efforts to remove vincible ignorance and would fault them (prudentially or morally) for not doing so.

Display 1.1. Types of ignorance

	One can remove	*One cannot remove*
One ought to remove	Culpable ignorance	(Case excluded)
One need not remove	Venial ignorance	Invincible (and thereby venial ignorance)

Note: Venial ignorance is always vincible. The inevitable (invariable) is never culpable (blameworthy). Invincibility is an effective excuse.

The distinction at issue accordingly has a significant ethical bearing. Since (by hypothesis) the mind of vincible ignorance lies in an individual's power, the voluntaries required for ethical or moral appraisal are present. Catholic theology, following the lead of St. Thomas Aquinas, condemns as a sin the vincible ignorance of those who—despite opportunity to the contrary—remain uninformed regarding the doctrines of the church.

Unavailable ignorance is ipso facto venial. And of course ignorance will always be both whenever it is inevitable.

The overall situation can be dependent as per display 1.1. It should be noted that invincible ignorance is always ipso facto venial: invincibility excuses—no culpability attaches to that which is inevitable and cannot be helped. But what of that which can be helped but only by extraordinary effort—ignorance that can indeed be removed but requires laborious inquiry or elaborate reasoning? St. Thomas Aquinas holds that this too diminishes culpability to a nullity.

There are four key sources of inevitable ignorance: unavailable factuality, statistical immorality, stochastic variability, and chaotic unpredictability. Accordingly, there are large areas of unknowing where the ignorance at issue is nowise culpable but rather inherent in the very nature of the realities within which the cognitive efforts of *Homo sapiens* have to unfold.

PRESUMPTION AS A GAP-FILLER FOR IGNORANCE

Nature abhors a vacuum. So does the human mind. We try not to let the gaps in our knowledge be mere empty blanks, so we fill them in with speculation and suppositions. The cognitive instrument that does the work here is presumption, which often serves as a placeholder for knowledge. For the reality of it is that we operate with a source of standard perceptions of presumption—of how to proceed in the absence of evidence to the contrary. These include such presumptions as conformity, normalcy, and symmetry, all of which envision having the things we do not know accord harmoniously with those that we do. (Nobody expected the other side of the moon to offer much beyond a variety of craters.)[7]

Ignorance is thus subject to a wide variety of presumptions. First is the universal that the people we encounter actually know the things that any normal intelligent person would be expected to know: that people need air to breathe, that stabbing people causes pain and does harm, etc. Other presumptions govern matters that people would be expected to know ex officio—as doctors, plumbers, babysitters, etc. Barring blue-ribbon excuses (going mad, sustaining brain damage, etc.), ignorance that rises counter to such presumptions is culpable: someone who exhibits ignorance here ought not to do so and is thereby guilty of a virtually ethical transgression. By contrast, ignorance is venial—understandable and excusable—when it exists in circumstances where there is no good reason why there should be any knowledge to the contrary. All of these things that people cannot possibly be expected to know—and, above all, those they cannot possibly know—afford instances of venial ignorance.

We standardly operate on the presumption of an absence of culpable ignorance—that people know the sorts of things which, under the circumstances, they ordinarily would and certainly should be aware of. For practical purposes we can convert the dictum that

"Ignorance of the law is no excuse" into an expanded counterpart: "Ignorance of readily available fact has no excuse."

THE EXTENT OF IGNORANCE

The situation of knowledge is not that of a crossword puzzle where the amount of what is unknown can somehow be measured in advance. We can form no sensible estimate of the imponderable domain of what can be known but is not.

Some writers analogize the cognitive exploration of the realm of fact to the geographic exploration of the earth. But this analogy is profoundly misleading. The earth has a finite and measurable surface, and so even when some part of it is unexplored, its magnitude and limits can be assessed in advance. Nothing of the kind obtains in the cognitive domain. The ratio and relationship of known truth to knowable fact is subject to no fixed and determinable proportion. Geographic exploration can expect eventual completeness, cognitive exploration cannot.

What is the extent of our ignorance? Just how vast is the domain of what we do not know? When confronted with these questions there lies before us the temptation of the analogy of global exploration with its property between "the known world," on the one hand, and the unexplained terra incognita, on the other. Now once it was grasped that the earth can be viewed as what is, at least roughly, a large sphere, it becomes possible to estimate its surface area and thereby to establish a proportion between the area of what has been explored and the unexamined remainder. But this picture of geographic knowledge is clearly missing in the case of knowledge at large. There just is no a priori way of measuring the size of the domain of *possible* knowledge in comparison with the domain of *available* knowledge. The idea of establishing a proportion here founders in the total infeasibility of making a here-and-now assessment of the extent of our ignorance.

That our knowledge is *pragmatically* sufficient for our immediate purposes—in enabling us to answer the questions that then and there confront us—is something that is in principle determinable. But that it is *theoretically* adequate to answer not just our present questions but those that will grow out of them in the course of future inquiry is something we can never manage to establish. To be sure, we can compare what one person or group knows with what some other person or group knows. But mapping the realm of what is knowable as such is beyond our powers.

There are, of course, finite fields of knowledge. There is only so much you can know (nonrelationally, at least) about the content of Boston's 1995 telephone directory—namely, the totality of what is in its pages. But that is only the case because here "what *can be* known" and "what is known" actually coincide. But this sort of thing is the case only in very special circumstances and never with respect to areas of natural science such as medicine or physics that deal with the products of nature at a level of generic generality.

Although ignorance lies at the core of this book, its deliberations are not an exercise in radical scepticism. It does not propose that knowledge about the world is unavailable to us. Instead, it contemplates that, despite whatever we may come to know, there are some matters about which we are destined to remain ignorant, and that among the things that we can get to know about are far-reaching facts about the nature and extent of our own ignorance.

WHY ARE WE SO IGNORANT?

Why can't we master a foreign language within a single week's effort or learn calculus in a fortnight? What explains our manifest cognitive deficiencies and limitations? Why don't we know a lot more than we do?[8]

This question is one that can in principle be answered in evolutionary terms.[9] But it has two importantly different aspects: (1) Why aren't we comprehensively smarter by way of enhanced mind power for the species as a whole, and (2) Why aren't we statistically smarter by way of an increase in the relative proportion of smart people within the presently constituted range of intelligence levels? Let us consider these issues one at a time.

To be a substantially smarter species, we would, for starters, need a much bigger brain on prevailing bioengineering principles. To manage this would require a larger—less agile—body, forcing us to forgo the advantages of maneuverability and versatility. To process twice the information would require a brain of roughly four times its present size. But to quadruple our brain weight we would need a body sixteen times its present weight.[10] A body of so great a weight is not only extremely cumbersome but involves enormous demands for energy. The most plausible and probable move would then be to opt for a very different ecological niche and take to the water, joining our mammalian cousins, the whales and dolphins. The stimulating surroundings of a land environment, with its invitations to communal socialization, division of labor, and technological development, would all be denied us. That gain in brain power would have come at an awesome cost, the sacrifice of the collective intelligence of the social institutionalization of tool-using creatures. The price is one that evolution cannot afford.[11]

There remains, however, the question of why we humans should not be smarter by way of a statistical improvement in the proportion of very smart people in our existing species. With this shift of questions, we now move from the issue of bioengineering a more intelligent species to the development of a more intelligent population—

one in which the percentage of people who would qualify as superior in intelligence by present standards would be substantially enlarged.

We humans are as smart as we are because we need to be so in order to function as the type of creature we have become. The reason why we are not a great deal smarter is not that "ignorance is bliss," but rather because a significantly higher level of intelligence would actually be biologically counterproductive—if not for the individual, then for the species. Indeed, it is far from clear that a confabulation of Einsteins would manage a human community better than one of "average Joes."

As long as the proportion of clever people in a society is fairly small, random interactive encounters will statistically occur among nonclever people. But in increasing the proportion of the clever, we also increase the chances of unequal encounters. Insofar as society benefits by harmonious interpersonal transactions, increasing the proportion of the clever would not advantage the group. Evolution would thus presumably militate against it.

The main benefit of smarts is learning by experience. But whether one is an individual or a species, experience adapts an individual to the prevailing conditions. And in a changing world, this can be far from beneficial. Another benefit of smarts is that of enabling individuals to get what they want more efficiently and effectively. But as every parent of a small child knows, what you want is not always what is good for you. There are many conditions and circumstances in which the processes and exercises of intelligence can be counterproductive.

If species endurance is the name of the game with regard to benefit, then the jury is still out on whether intelligence is all that advantageous. Dinosaurs may well outperform *Homo sapiens* in this regard, not to speak of cockroaches. And if proliferation is the name of the game, we are not even in the same league with ants.

Moreover, the social dimension of the matter also comes into play here. Consider the following sort of case. You and I interact in a competitive situation of potential benefit that has a roughly zero-sum character, with one party's gain as the other's loss. Two alternatives are open to each of us to collaborate with the other, or to try to outwit him. If we collaborate, we shall share the resultant benefit (say by each getting one-half). If we compete, then the winner takes all; whoever succeeds gains the whole benefit. The overall situation thus stands as depicted in display 1.2.

Display 1.2. Hypothetical payoffs in a situation of competition

	Fortune favors me	*Fortune favors you*
We collaborate	0.5 B / 0.5 B	0.5 B / 0.5 B
We fail to collaborate	B / 0	0 / B

Note: The table entry *B* represents the gains for the two parties you and me, respectively.

If I see my chances of winning as given by the probability p, then my expectations stand as follows:

$$\text{EV (collaborate)} = p\,(0.5\ B) + (1-p)\,(0.5\ B) = 0.5\ B$$
$$\text{EV (compete)} = p\,(B) + (1-p)\,(0) = p\,(B)$$

So long as p is less than one-half—that is, as long as my subjectively appraised chances of winning are less than even—collaboration is the sensible course relative to the balance of expectations. But when p exceeds one-half, the balance moves in favor of noncooperation. If one views the benefits of self-reliance optimistically, then decision-theoretic rationality inclines against cooperation; it favors going one's own competitive way and taking one's chances. On the other hand, people who see themselves as comparatively more clever are less likely to collaborate.

Overall, two counterbalancing forces are operative: the one a primarily natural tendency toward increasing the proportions of the highly able, and the other a primarily social tendency toward the maintenance of a cooperation-compelling diversity. If we humans were by and large smarter, we would, no doubt, be able to manage various interactions with nature somewhat more successfully. Our ability to manipulate our environment cognitively and physically—to explain, predict, control—would be enhanced. But our interactions with one another would be subject to an increased temptation for people to try to outsmart their fellows. Rational calculation regarding potentially competitive interactions would not favor the course of competition, of trying to outwit. The socially beneficial impetus to cooperation becomes undermined. In a way, statistical inferiority serves as an equalizer. And this is all to the general good. The natural outrage we feel, even as children, against noncooperation and people who do not play fair is patently connected in the evolutionary order with the fact that most of us draw substantial benefits from a system in which people play by the rules. Accordingly, if humans were proportionately more intelligent than we are, there would be fewer chances of socially benign encounters.

As the bee illustrates, the evolution of cooperation certainly does not require individual intelligence. Quite to the contrary. As the number of clever people who pride themselves on strength of intellect increases, social cohesion becomes more difficult to obtain. University faculties are notoriously difficult to manage. Experts are thorns in the sides of popes and presidents alike: no sect manages to keep on easy terms with its theologians. (Anyone who is familiar with the ways of an intellectual avant-garde—such as the Bloomsbury circle—has some idea of the difficulties of socializing people who see themselves as more than ordinarily clever.) It is easy to envision how in numerous circumstances intelligence militates against socially benign cooperation.

These deliberations yield the odd-sounding lesson that evolutionary pressure is a two-edged sword that can act in opposed directions concerning the development of intelligence. Evolution is a process in which the balance of cost and benefit is constantly maintained in a delicate equilibrium. And this general phenomenon is vividly illustrated in the particular case of our cognitive capacities. On the one hand, we humans are not less intelligent than we are, because if we were, we would incur an evolutionary disadvantage in our physical dealings with nature. But analogously, we are not more intelligent than we are, because if we were, we would also suffer an evolutionary disability by becoming disadvantaged in our social dealings with one another, since we would no longer feel constrained to cooperate, because the course of events drives home the recognition that we are just not smart enough to go it alone. In its handling of intelligence, evolution, like a shrewd gambler, is clever enough to follow the precept "Quit while you're ahead."

IS IGNORANCE A MISFORTUNE?

Notwithstanding the dictum that "Ignorance is bliss," most would agree that it is, in fact, something of a misfortune.[12] True, for the most part ignorance is unfortunate and regrettable. But not always! There is some modicum of justice to the saying that "Ignorance is bliss." For human life being what it is would bring a full quota of misfortunes to oneself and those one holds dear. And prior knowledge of such developments would greatly augment their distressing impact. The joys of the present would be overshadowed by the anticipations of misfortunes to come. And in other cases where precognition indicates not mishaps as such but merely increased risks, we would often undergo needless worry about misfortunes that may very possibly never arrive. Thus it very much depends whether ignorance is something fortunate or unfortunate. That a terrorist does not know how to make a bomb is fortunate, that he knows where to obtain the necessary materials is not. The status of knowledge in point of positivity/negativity depends not so much on the information as such but on what is done with it.[13]

A HISTORICAL EXCURSUS

Scepticism apart, the most developed theory of ignorance in modern philosophy is that of Immanuel Kant. In his classic *Critique of Pure Reason* (1781), Kant maintained that, while we can know the things we encounter in our experiential interactions with the world's realities, those realities as such (the realm of "things in themselves") are inherently unknowable to us. Accordingly, Kant opened his *Critique of Pure Reason* with the following thesis:

> Human reason has this peculiar fate that in one species of its knowledge it is burdened by questions which, as prescribed by the very nature of reason itself, it is not able to ignore, but which, as transcending all its powers, it is also not able to answer. (Avii).

He was convinced that:

> In the explanation of natural appearances, on the other hand, much must remain uncertain and many questions insoluble, because what we know of nature is by no means sufficient, in all cases, to account for what has to be explained. (A477/B505)

And Kant was eager to present various concrete examples of such unamenable questions and irresolvable issues.

> This peculiarity of our understanding, that it can produce *a priori* unity of apperception solely by means of the categories, and only by such and so many, is as little capable

of further explanation as why we have just these and no
other functions of [informative] judgment, or why space
and time are the only forms of our possible [sensory]
intuition. (B146)

In particular, why the content (as distinguished from the form) of
our sensations and cognitions are as they are—their intelligible basis,
or *Grund,* as Kant terms it—is an impenetrable mystery for us.

The non-sensible cause of these representations is completely unknown to us, and cannot thereby be regarded
as an object. (A494/B522)

And again:

The relation of our sensibility to an object and what the
transcendental ground of its [objective] unity may be,
are matters undoubtedly so deeply concealed that we,
who after all know even ourselves only through inner
sense and therefore as appearance, can never be justified
in treating sensibility as being a suitable instrument of
investigation for discovering anything save always still
other appearances—eager as we yet are to explore their
non-sensible cause. (A278/B334)

And again:

The much-discussed question of the communion between the thinking and the extended, if we leave aside all
that is merely fictitious, comes then simply to this: *how in
a thinking subject outer intuition*, namely, that of space, with
its filling-in of shape and motion, *is possible.* And this is a
question which no man can possibly answer. This gap in
our knowledge can never be filled; all that can be done
is to indicate it through the ascription of outer appear-

ances to that transcendental object which is the cause of
this species of representations, but of which we can have
no knowledge whatsoever and of which we shall never
acquire any concept. (A393)

 What things are in themselves—above and beyond the limitations of
our experience—is inaccessible to our thought:

> The employment of our categories can never extend fur-
> ther than to the objects of experience. Doubtless, indeed,
> there are intelligible entities corresponding to the sensible
> entities; there may also be intelligible entities to which
> our sensible faculty of intuition has no relation what-
> soever; but our concepts of understanding, being mere
> forms of thought for our sensible intuition, could not in
> the least apply to them. (B309)

And again:

> [Our understanding] does indeed think for itself an object
> in itself . . . which is the cause of appearance and there-
> fore not itself appearance. . . . We are completely ignorant
> whether it is to be met within us or outside us, whether it
> would be at once removed with the cessation of sensibil-
> ity, or whether in the absence sensibility it would still
> remain (A288/B345)

And again:

> I cannot say, therefore, that the world is *infinite* in space
> or as regards past time. Any such concept of magnitude,
> as being that of a given infinitude, is empirically impos-
> sible, and therefore, in reference to the world as an object
> of the senses, also absolutely impossible. . . . I also cannot
> say that the regress is *finite*; an absolute limit is likewise

empirically impossible. Thus I can say nothing regarding the whole object of experience, the world of sense. (A520/B548)

As Kant saw it, it is the tragic fate of human reason that it cannot escape from questions which it is inherently unable to resolve—not because those questions are in themselves meaningless, but because posing them is (literally) unreasonable in asking of human reason that which, by its very nature, it cannot possibly do.

And so:

> Whether the world has a beginning [in time] and any limit to its extension in space; whether there is anywhere, and perhaps in my thinking self, an indivisible and indestructible unity, or nothing but what is divisible and transitory; whether I am free in my actions or, like other beings, am led by the hand of nature and of fate; whether finally there is a supreme cause of the world . . . these are questions for the solution of which the mathematician would gladly exchange the whole of his science. For mathematics can yield no satisfaction in regard to those highest ends that most closely concern humanity. (A463–64/B491–92)

Thus for Kant the factors or forces that productively engender the dramaturgy of our experiences are matters to which we human knowers can have no cognitive access: ours is a world of *phenomena* that has a merely empirical or experiential reality whose underlying ontological or metaphysical basis is transcendental through transcending the reach of our cognitive capacities.

The Scottish philosopher James Ferrier took matters a step further than Kant.[14] Subscribing to the Principle of Sufficient Reason *(Satz vom Grunde)*, Kant does not question that we stand committed to the idea of a nonphenomenal ground *(a ratio essendi)* for the phenomena, a ground which, by its very nature as such, is unknown. Ferrier, by contrast, insists that nescience is not ignorance: that one can be ignorant only where knowledge is in theory possible:

> Ignorance, properly so called—that is, the ignorance which is a defect—must not be confounded with . . . a nescience of that which it would contradict the nature of intelligence to know. Such a nescience is no defect or imperfection—it is, on the contrary, the very strength or perfection of reason; and therefore such nescience is not to be regarded as ignorance.[15]

One can be ignorant, Ferrier holds, only of that which can be known, and since "things in themselves" are beyond the reach of possible knowledge by finite beings, we cannot be said to be ignorant of them. As Ferrier sees it, "things in themselves" are not a subject for meaningful claims, since such claims are by nature confined to matters regarding that of which we can achieve knowledge.

For Ferrier, *ignorance* was a pejorative term. He sought to deploy the neutral term *nescience* from the mode of unknowing as an issue with a principled and inescapable incapacity to resolve certain questions. Between the lines of Ferrier's "agnosiology" is the conviction that one cannot speak informatively about unknowables, and whereof one cannot meaningfully speak, one must remain silent. In this context, however, Ferrier was by no means a sceptic. For as he saw it, we can certainly achieve knowledge—at any rate, about the limits of knowledge itself.

Against those of the Leibniz-Wolff School whom he denounced as "dogmatists," Kant maintained—on basically empiricist principles—that the ultimate ground of existence is ultimately unknowable for us. Be this correct or not—and it is certainly arguable—the fact remains that one must, with Ferrier, distinguish between the nescience of inevitable unknowing and the contingency of an in-principle separable ignorance. And one must acknowledge that, from the theoretical and philosophical point of view, it is the issue of an in-principle insuperable ignorance that occupies the forefront of interest.

Questions and Insolubilia

It is instructive to take an erotetic—that is, question-oriented—view of knowledge and ignorance. After all, someone knows that p when (and only when) they can *cogently* give a correct answer to the question "Is p the case?" and an answer is given cogently when (and only when) the giver has a satisfactory *rationale* for giving it.

There are two possibilities for erotetic ignorance: (1) generic question-resolving incapacity ("There is some question Q that one cannot answer") and (2) concrete question-resolving incapacity ("Q is a specific, here-and-now identifiable question that one cannot answer").[1] Even as there is concrete and indefinite knowledge, so there is concrete and generic ignorance as well. But there is a crucial difference here. For in the case of questions—unlike factual knowledge—we can be concretely specific regarding our incapacity. We cannot coherently say "p is a specific truth (fact) I do not know." But saying "Q is a specific question I cannot answer" is altogether unproblematic.

When we look at cognition from the angle of questions rather than that of knowledge, ignorance becomes identifiable. Erotetic ignorance—the inability to answer questions—is accordingly something quite different from propositional ignorance: the failure to know truths. For with erotetic ignorance we can hope to get beyond generalities to identify questions that we cannot answer. But this sort of specificity is something that we cannot manage in the realm of propositional knowledge.

KANT'S PRINCIPLE

New knowledge emerging from the progress of science can bear very differently on the matter of questions. Specifically, in the course of cognitive progress we can discover the following:

1. New (that is, *different*) answers to old questions.
2. New questions.
3. The inappropriateness or illegitimacy of old questions.

With 1 we learn that the wrong answer has been given to an old question: we uncover an error of commission in our previous question-answering endeavors. With 2 we discover that there are certain questions which have not heretofore been posed at all: we uncover an error of omission in our former question-asking endeavors. Finally, with 3 we find that one has asked the wrong question altogether: we uncover an error of commission in our former question-asking endeavors, which are now seen to rest on incorrect presuppositions (and are thus generally bound up with type 1 discoveries). Three rather different sorts of cognitive progress are thus involved here—different from one another and from the traditional view of cognitive progress in terms of a straightforward "accretion of further knowledge."

The coming to be and passing away of questions are phenomena that can be mooted on this basis. A question *arises* at the time t if it then can meaningfully be posed because all its presuppositions are then taken to be true. And a question *dissolves* at t if one or another of its previously accepted presuppositions is no longer accepted. Any state of science will remove certain questions from the agenda and dismiss them as inappropriate. Newtonian dynamics dismissed the question, "What cause is operative to keep a body in movement (with a uniform velocity in a straight line) once an impressed force has set it into motion?" Modern quantum theory does not allow us to ask, "What caused this atom on californium to disintegrate after exactly 32.53 days, rather than, say, a day or two later?" Scientific questions should thus be regarded as arising in a *historical* setting. They arise at some juncture and not at others; they can be born and then die away.

A change of mind about the appropriate answer to some question will unravel the entire fabric of questions that presupposed this earlier answer. For if we change our mind regarding the correct answer to one member of a chain of questions, then the whole of a subsequent course of questioning may well collapse. If we abandon the luminiferous ether as a vehicle for electromagnetic radiation, then we lose at one stroke the whole host of questions about its composition, structure, mode of operation, origin, and so on.

Epistemic change over time thus relates not only to what is "*known*" but also to what can be *asked*. The accession of "new knowledge" opens up new questions. And when the epistemic status of a presupposition changes from acceptance to abandonment or rejection, we witness the disappearance of various old ones through dissolution. Questions regarding the modus operandi of phlogiston, the behavior of caloric fluid, the structure of the luminiferous ether, and the character of faster-than-light transmissions are all questions that have become lost to modern science because they involve presuppositions that have been abandoned.

The second of those three modes of erotetic discovery is particularly significant. The phenomenon of the ever-continuing "birth" of new questions was first emphasized by Immanuel Kant, who saw the development of natural science in terms of a continually evolving cycle of questions and answers, where *"every answer given on principles of experience begets a fresh question, which likewise requires its answer* and thereby clearly shows the insufficiency of all scientific modes of explanation to satisfy reason."[2] This claim suggests the following Principle of Question Propagation—Kant's Principle, as we shall call it: "The answering of our factual (scientific) questions always paves the way to further as yet unanswered questions."

An important lesson emerges. In overcoming ignorance by securing answers to our questions in the course of inquiry we do not reduce the overall volume of identifiable ignorance in terms of the number of visible questions to which we lack answers.

LIMITATIONS VERSUS BOUNDARIES (*SCHRANKEN/GRENZEN*)

The situation regarding our cognitive limits in the light of question-resolving incapacities is not quite as bleak as it may seem. For even though the thought and knowledge of finite beings are destined to be ever incomplete, they nevertheless have no fixed and determinate limits. Consider an analogy in counting integers: there is a limit beyond which we never *will* get, but there is no limit beyond which we never *can* get. The line of thought operative in these deliberations was already mooted by Kant:

> In natural philosophy, human reason admits of *limits* ("excluding limits," *Schranken*) but not of *boundaries* ("terminating limits," *Grenzen*), namely, it admits that something indeed lies without it, at which it can never arrive, but not that it will at any point find completion in

> its internal progress . . . . [T]he possibility of new discov-
> eries is infinite: and the same is the case with the discov-
> ery of new properties of nature, of new powers and laws
> by continued experience and its rational combination.[3]

The fact that ignorance is ineliminable in the larger scheme of things does not stand in the way of answering any or many of the particular questions in which we take an interest. While ignorance is indeed here to stay, it will never block the path to progress.

And so, while our cognitive limitedness as finite beings is real enough, there nevertheless are no boundaries—no *determinate* limits—to the manifold of discoverable fact. And here Kant was right. For while the cognitive range of finite beings is indeed limited, it is also boundless because it is not limited in a way that blocks the prospect of cognitive access to ever new and ongoingly more informative facts that afford us an ever ampler and more adequate account of reality.[4]

UNIDENTIFIABILITY AND VAGRANT PREDICATES

A peculiar and interesting mode of reference occurs when an item is referred to obliquely *in such a way that its specific identification is flat out precluded as a matter of principle.* This phenomenon is illustrated by claims to the existence of the following:

- A thing whose identity will never be known
- An idea that never occurs to anybody
- An occurrence that no one ever mentions
- An integer that is never individually specified

There are certainly bound to be such things, but we obviously cannot identify them.[5] In these cases, those particular items that render

"Some x has F" true are *referentially inaccessible:* to indicate them individually and specifically as instances of the predicate at issue is ipso facto to unravel them as so-characterized items.[6]

The concept of a predicate that is somehow applicable but nevertheless noninstantiable comes to view at this point. We have a predicate F whose realization is noninstantiable because, while it is true *in abstracto* that this property is exemplified—that is, $(\exists u)Fu$ will be true—nevertheless the very manner of its specification makes it impossible to identify any particular individual u_0 such that Fu_0 obtains. Such predicates are "vagrant" in the sense of *having no known address or fixed abode:* though they indeed have applications, these cannot be specifically instanced—they cannot be pinned down and located in a particular spot. Accordingly, we may define the following:

> F is a *vagrant* predicate iff $(\exists x)Fx$ is true, while nevertheless
> Fx_0 is false for each and every specifically identified u_0.[7]

Predicates of this sort will be such that one can show on the basis of general principles that there must be items to which they apply, while nevertheless it can be shown that no such items can ever be concretely identified.[8] While the predicates indeed have application, we are destined to be ignorant about where they apply.[9]

The following predicates represent properties that are clearly noninstantiable in this way, by being:

- An ever-unstated proposition (or theory, contention, etc.)
- A never-mentioned topic (or idea, object, etc.)
- A truth (a fact) no one ever realizes (or learns, or states)
- Someone whom everyone has forgotten
- A never-identified culprit
- An issue no one has thought about since the sixteenth century

Noninstantiability itself is certainly not something that is noninstantiable: many instances of it are readily adduced.

Vagrant predicates are by nature noninstantiable, but we can nevertheless use them to *individuate* items that we can never *identify*. Consider "the oldest unknown (i.e., never-to-be identified) victim of the eruption of Krakatoa. We can clearly make various true claims about the so-individuated person—for example, that he or she was alive at the time of Krakatoa's eruption. Reference is no problem here. But by hypothesis we cannot manage to identify the individual. Predicative vagrancy thus reinforces the distinction between mere individuation and actual identification.

The existence of vagrant predicates shows that applicability and instantiability do not come to the same thing. By definition, vagrant predicates will be applicable. But this is always something that must be claimed on the basis of general principles; doing so by means of concretely identified instances is, by hypothesis, infeasible.

Consider an example of this sort of general-principle demonstration. There are infinitely many positive integers. But the earth has a beginning and end in time. And its overall history has room for only a finite number of intelligent earthlings, each of whom can only make specific mention of a finite number of integers. (They can, of course, refer to the set of integers at large, but they can only specifically take note of some finite number of them.) There will accordingly be some ever-unmentioned, ever-unconsidered integers—indeed, an infinite number of them. But clearly no one can give a specific example of this. (The substitutional interpretation of quantifiers will not work with these vagrant predicates.) Or, again, consider being an unstated proposition.

In the history of the species there can only be a finite number of specifically stated propositions, while actual truths must be infinite in number; therefore, we know that there will be some such unstatable. But to say specifically of a *particular* proposition that *it* is unstated is impracticable. We can allude to such items generically, but we cannot actually identify them specifically.

In sum, then, vagrant predicates reflect a salient cognitive incapacity where such materials are at issue: we can ascertain *that* such predicates apply but not *where* they do so. Ignorance is inevitable here.

VAGRANT PREDICATES AS EPISTEMIC

In theoretical matters of logic or mathematics—where predicates cast in the language of cognitive operators have no place—one never encounters vagrant predicates. For in such contexts we affirm *what* we know but never claim *that* we know. However, with epistemic matters the situation can be very different.

Consider such predicates as these:

- Being a tree no one has ever seen
- Being a sunset never witnessed by any member of *Homo sapiens*

Such items may be difficult to instantiate—but certainly not impossible. The former could be instantiated by positional coordinates, the latter by place and date. In neither case will an instantiation unravel that item as described. Being seen is not indispensably essential to trees, nor to sunsets: being an unseen tree or being an unwitnessed sunset involves no contradiction in terms. But in those epistemic cases that concern us now, epistemic inaccessibility is built into the specification at issue. Here being instantiated stands in direct logico-conceptual conflict with the characterization at issue, as with the following:

- Being a person who has passed into total oblivion
- Being a never-formulated question
- Being an idea no one any longer mentions

To identify such an item (in the way now at issue) is thereby to un-ravel its specifying characterization.[10] The application and instruc-tion of such predicates fall into what deserves to be characterized as a cognitive blindspot.[11]

The involvement of knowledge is of the essence here. What is pivotal in all of these cases of vagrant predicates is that they involve a specification which—like identification, comprehension, formula-tion, mention, etc.—is fundamentally epistemic, something that can only be performed by a creature capable of cognitive and communi-cative performances. This is readily established. Let F be a vagrant predicate. Since we then by hypothesis have it that $(\exists u)Fu$ is true, there is clearly nothing impossible about being F-possessing as such. Ontologically speaking, there are, by hypothesis, items to which F applies; what is infeasible is only providing an instance—a specific example or illustration. The impossibility lies not in "being an F" as such but in "being a concretely instantiated F." The problem is not with the indefinite "*something* is an F" but with the specific "*this* is an F." Difficulty lies not with F-hood as such, but with its specific application—not with the ontology of there being an F, but with the epistemology of its apprehension in individual cases.

The salient point is that specification and exemplification are epistemic processes that, as such, are incompatible with those epis-temically voided characterizations provided by vagrant predicates. Total oblivion and utter nonentertainment are automatically at odds with identificatory instantiation. After all, honoring a request to identify the possessor of an noninstantiable property is simply im-possible. For any such response would be self-defeating.

It is this uniting, common feature of all vagrant predicates that they are so specified that in the very act of identifying a would-be instantiation of them we will automatically violate—that is, falsify—one of the definitive features of the specification at issue. In other words, with such noninstantiable features their noninstantiability is something inherent in the defining specification of the features at issue.

The very concept of instantiability/noninstantiability is thus epistemic in its bearing because all of the relevant procedures—exemplifying, illustrating, identifying, naming, and the like—are inherently referential by way of purporting a knowledge of identity. And since all such referential processes are mind-projected—and cannot but be so—they are epistemic in nature. And so the idea of knowledge is unavoidably present throughout the phenomenon of predicative vagrancy, seeing that the factor of ignorance is essential here. Vagrant predicates always involve ignorance. And this inevitable ignorance at issue with the institution of vagrant predicates is accordingly just another aspect of our inevitable ignorance regarding the reach of ignorance itself.

INSOLUBILIA AND PROBLEMATIC QUESTIONS

Vagrant predicates open the doorway to unanswerable questions. To be sure, *answering* a question is not simply a matter of giving a response that happens to be correct. For a proper answer must not only be correct but also credible: it must have the backing of a rationale that renders its correctness evident. For example, take the question whether the mayor of San Antonio had eggs for breakfast yesterday. You say yes; I say no. Though neither of us has a clue, one of us is bound to be right. But neither one of us has managed to provide a real answer to the question. One of us has made a verbal response that happens to be correct, but neither of us has given a cognitively appropriate answer in the sense of the term that is now at issue. To qualify as an *answer* there must be not only a response but a response that is, under the circumstances, manifestly acceptable. And this would require the backing of a cogent rationale of credibility; merely to guess at an answer, for example, or to draw it out of a hat, is not really to answer the question.

The medieval schoolmen understood by "insolubilia" such self-refuting propositions as that of the Liar Paradox ("What I am saying is false") or that of self-contradiction ("There are no truths"). However, the term eventually came to cover a wider spectrum of examples—all related to puzzle situations where it is difficult to see on which alternate side the truth of the matter lies.[12]

We shall not be concerned here with ill-formed questions that suffer from some sort of inherent defect. Thus paradox is out, and self-invalidating questions such as, "Why is this question unintelligible?" must be put aside. And so must the inquiry, "How many rocks are there in Africa?" seeing that the problem here is that it is totally unclear what it is to count as being a rock. Is a grain of sand a rock? Is a stony mountain outcropping a rock? The question evaporates in a fog of imprecision.

Moreover, a question can also be ill-formed in that it somehow involves an inappropriate presupposition. Consider "What is one-third of the prime number between 7 and 11?" There just isn't any such prime. The question self-destructs by asking for something whose nonexistence can be established and thereby rests on false presupposition.

A further version of question meaninglessness is provided by *paradoxical* questions—that is, questions such that *every* possible answer is false. An instance is afforded by a yes/no question that cannot be answered correctly, such as, "When you respond to this question, will the answer be negative?" Consider the possibilities in display 2.1.

Display 2.1. Paradoxical questions

Answer given	Truth status of the answer
Yes	False
No	False

On this basis, that query emerges as meaningless through representing a paradoxical question that cannot be answered correctly. Inability to answer an inappropriate question cannot be seen as betokening ignorance. For, properly speaking, this obtains only when one does not know the correct answer to an appropriate question.

Only meaningful questions that do indeed have correct answers will concern us here. There are, of course, also questions that cannot be answered incorrectly; for example, "What is an example of something that someone has given an example of?" Any *possible* answer to this question will thereby be correct. Inability to answer such a question would betoken not so much ignorance as idiocy.

UNANSWERABLE QUESTIONS

While we cannot cite facts we do not know, we can certainly identify questions we cannot answer. But when we look at cognition from the angle of questions rather than knowledge, ignorance becomes concretely identifiable. As we have seen, it is impossible to give an instance of a truth that no one knows. But questions that no one can possibly answer correctly can indeed be found. It is instructive to pursue this prospect.

In inquiring into this problem area, we are not interested in questions whose unanswerability resides merely in the contingent fact that certain information is not in practice accessible. "Did Julius Caesar hear a dog bark on his thirtieth birthday?" There is no possible way in which we can secure the needed information here and now. (Time travel is still impracticable.) But of course such questions are not inherently unanswerable, and it is unanswerability as a matter of principle that concerns us here.[13]

Now some questions are unanswerable for essentially practical reasons: we lack any prospect of finding effective means for their resolution, for reasons of contingent fact—the impracticability of time travel, say, or of space travel across the vast reaches involved. But such contingently grounded ignorance is not as bad as it gets. For some questions are in principle irresoluble in that purely theoretical reasons (rather than mere practical limitations) preclude the possibility of securing the information required for their resolution. There are—or may be—no sound reasons for dismissing such questions as meaningless because hypothetical beings can be imagined by whom such a question can be resolved. But given the inevitabilities of *our* situation as time-bound and finite intelligences, the question may be such that any prospect of resolution is precluded on grounds of general principle.

But are there any such questions? Are there some issues regarding which we are condemned to ignorance?

There are two principal sorts of meaningfully unanswerable questions, those that are *locally* irresolvable and those that are *globally* irresolvable. Locally unanswerable questions are those which a particular individual or group is unable to answer. An instance of such a question is: "What is an example of a fact of which you are altogether ignorant?" Clearly you cannot possibly manage to answer this, because whatever you adduce as such a fact must be something you know or believe to be such (that is, a fact), so that you cannot possibly be altogether ignorant of it. On the other hand, it is clear that *somebody else* could readily be in the position to answer the question. Again, consider such questions as the following:

- What is an example of a problem that will never be considered by any human being?
- What is an example of an idea that will never occur to any human being?

There are sound reasons of general principle (the potential infinitude of problems and ideas; the inherent finitude of human intelligence) to hold that the items at issue in these questions (problems that will never be considered; ideas that will never occur) do actually exist. And it seems altogether plausible to think that other (nonhuman) hypothetically envisionable intelligences could well answer these questions correctly, although it is equally clear that we humans could never provide the requisite answers.

And looking beyond this we can also contemplate the prospect of globally intractable questions such that nobody (among finite intelligences at least) can possibly be in a position to answer them (in the strict sense described at the outset). These questions have an appropriate answer, but for reasons of general principle no one—no finite intelligence at least—can possibly be in a position to provide it.[14]

An example of such globally unanswerable questions can be provided by nontrivial but inherently uninstantiable predicates along the lines of the following:

- What idea is there that will never again occur to anybody?
- What occurrence is there that no one ever mentions?

There undoubtedly are such items, but of course they cannot be instantiated, so that questions which ask for examples here are inherently unanswerable.[15]

INSTANTIATING INSOLUBILIA

The questions that will now concern us are those that are both answer-possessing and unanswerable. If such questions can indeed be adduced, then, while one cannot identify an *unknown* truth, one would be able to identify cases of *unspecifiable* truth, propositions such that either p_0 or not-p_0 must be true and yet nevertheless there is no prospect of determining which it is. Here we can localize truth by placing it within a limited range (one here consisting of p_0 and $\sim p_0$), but we cannot pinpoint it within this range of alternatives. One member of the assertion/denial pair will unquestionably prove to be true. And so one way or the other a case of truth stands before us. It's just that we cannot possibly say which member of the pair it is: the specifics of the matters are unknowable.

But are there such unanswerable questions? To begin with, there is the prospect of what might be called the *weak limitation* inherent in the circumstance that there are certain issues on its agenda that science cannot resolve *now*. However, this condition of weak limitation is perfectly compatible with the circumstance that *every* question that can be raised at this stage will *eventually* be answered at a future juncture. And so, a contrasting way in which the question-resolving capacity of our knowledge may be limited can envisage the more drastic situation: strong-limitation (the existence of insolubilia). There will (as of some juncture) be then-posable questions which will *never* obtain answers, meaningful questions whose resolution lies beyond the reach of science altogether—questions that will remain ever unsolved on the cognitive agenda. We are able to bring to realization such strong limitation of the existence of immoral questions—permanently unanswerable questions (general insolubilia) that admit of no resolution within any cognitive corpus.

However, for there to be *insolubilia*, it is certainly not necessary that anything be said about the current *availability* of the insoluble question. The prospect of its actual identification *at this or indeed any other particular prespecified historical juncture is wholly untouched.* Even a position that holds that there indeed *are* insolubilia certainly need not regard them as being identifiable at the present state-of-the-art scientific development. One can accordingly also move beyond the two preceding theses to the even stronger principle of hyperlimitation (the existence of *identifiable* insolubilia). Our present-day cognitive agenda includes certain here-and-now specifiable and scientifically meaningful questions whose resolution lies beyond the reach of science altogether. Awkwardly, however, a claim to identify insolubilia by pinpointing here and now issues that future inquiry will never resolve can readily go awry. Charles S. Peirce has put the key point trenchantly:

> For my part, I cannot admit the proposition of Kant—that there are certain impassable bounds to human knowledge. . . . The history of science affords illustrations enough of the folly of saying that this, that, or the other can never be found out. Auguste Comte said that it was clearly impossible for man ever to learn anything of the chemical constitution of the fixed stars, but before his book had reached its readers the discovery which he had announced as impossible had been made. Legendre said of a certain proposition in the theory of numbers that, while it appeared to be true, it was most likely beyond the powers of the human mind to prove it; yet the next writer on the subject gave six independent demonstrations of the theorem.[16]

To identify an insoluble problem, we would have to show that a certain inherently appropriate question is such that its resolution lies beyond every (possible or imaginable) state of future science. This task is clearly a rather tall order. Its realization is clearly difficult. But not in principle impossible.

And so the question, "Are there nondecidable scientific questions regarding nature's ways that scientific inquiry will *never* resolve—even were it to continue ad infinitum" represents an insolubilism that cannot possibly ever be settled in a decisive way. After all, how could we possibly establish that a question Q about some issue of fact will continue to be raisable and unanswerable in every future state of science, seeing that we cannot now circumscribe the changes that science might undergo in the future? And, since this is so, we have it—rather interestingly—that this question itself is self-instantiating: in being itself a question regarding an aspect of reality (of which of course science itself is a part) that scientific inquiry will never—at any specific state of the art—be in a position to settle decisively. We are cognitively myopic with respect to future knowledge. It is in principle infeasible for us to tell now how future science will answer present questions, or even what questions will figure on the question agenda of the future, let alone what answers they will engender. In this regard, as in others, it lies in the inevitable realities of our cognitive condition that the detailed nature of our ignorance is—for us at least—hidden away in an impenetrable fog of obscurity.

But of course insoluble questions relate to the issue of knowledge, whereas the very impredictability of future knowledge renders the identification of noncognitive scientific *insolubilia* impracticable. The limits of one's information set unavoidable limits to one's predictive capacities. In particular, we cannot foresee what we cannot conceive. Our questions—let alone answers—cannot outreach the limited horizons of our concepts.

To elaborate the prospect of identifying unknowable truth, let us consider once more the issue of future scientific knowledge—and specifically upon the already mooted issue of the historicity of knowledge. And in this light let us consider a thesis *(T)* on the order of the following: As long as scientific inquiry continues in our universe, there will *always* be a time when *some* then-unresolved (but resolvable) questions on the scientific agenda of the day will be sufficiently difficult to remain unresolved for at least two years.

What is at issue here is clearly a matter of fact—one way or the other. But now let Q be the question: "Is T true or not?" It is clear that actually to answer this question Q one way or the other, we would need to have cognitive access to the question agenda of all future times. And emphasized above, in relation to theses of the *always/some* format—whose negation would run *sometimes/all*—are bound to be problematic for finite knowers because of the unusuality that is involved either way. Accordingly, just this sort of information about future knowledge is something that we cannot manage to achieve. By their very nature as such, the discoveries of the future are unavailable at present, and in consequence Q^* affords an example of an insolubilium—a specific and perfectly meaningful question that we shall always and ever be unable to resolve decisively—irrespective of what the date on the calendar happens to read.

Nevertheless, the issue is certainly one that lies open to reasonable conjecture—something which, of course, is very far from achieving *knowledge*. For as viewed in the light of the present deliberations thesis T is altogether plausible—it has all the earmarks of a likely truth.[17] And so it seems reasonable to hold that conjectures of the sort at issue with proposition T above are the best and most that we can hope to do, given that assured knowledge about the future of science is simply unattainable.[18]

Cognitive Shortfall

STATEMENTS ARE ENUMERABLE, AS ARE TRUTHS

Ironically, one of the prime limitations of our knowledge is inherent in the very nature of language, its essential and most powerful instrumentality. Twentieth-century philosophers of otherwise the most radically different orientation have agreed on prioritizing the role of language. "The limits of my language set the limits of my world" (Die Grenzen meiner Spache bedeuten die Grenzen meiner Welt), says the Wittgenstein of the *Tractatus* (at 5.6). "There is nothing outside text" (Il n'y a pas de hors de texte), say the devotees of French deconstructionism. But already centuries earlier Leibniz had taken the measure of this sort of logocentrism. He viewed it up close and saw that it could not be sustained.[1]

Even if one construes the idea of an "alphabet" sufficiently broadly to include not only letters but also symbols of various sorts, it still holds that everything statable in a language can be spelled out in print through the combinational concatenation of some sequential register

of symbols.[2] And with a "language" construed as calling for development in the usual recursive manner, it transpires that the statements
of a language can be enumerated in a vast and indeed infinite but
nevertheless ultimately countable listing.[3] But since the world's languages, even if not finite in number, are enumerable, it follows that
the set of all statements—including every linguistically formidable
proposition—will be *enumerably* infinite (and thus have the transfi-
nite cardinality that mathematicians designate as *alef-zero*).

As a matter of principle, then, we obtain:

THESIS 1: THE ENUMERABILITY OF STATEMENTS

Statements (linguistically formulated propositions) are
enumerable and thus (at most) denumerably infinite.

Our linguistic resources for describing concrete states of affairs are
thus subject to quantitative limitation. And insofar as our thoughts
about things proceed by recursively developed linguistic means it is
inherently limited in its reach within the confines of countability.
And so the upshot is that the limits of textuality impose quantitative limitations upon propositionalized thought—albeit not limits of
finitude.

Unstatable truth is a contradiction in terms. Truths are inherently
linguistic in character, and thereby bound indissolubly to textuality.
And any language-framed declaration can be generated recursively
from a sequential string of symbols—seeing, that all spoken language can in principle be reduced to writing. On this basis, it follows
that truths cannot be more than countably infinite. And on this basis
we have:

THESIS 2: THE DENUMERABILITY OF TRUTH

While the manifold of the truth cannot be finitely inven-
toried, truths are nevertheless no more than denumerable
infinite in number.

THE INEXHAUSTIBILITY OF FACT: FACTS ARE TRANSDENUMERABLE

It serves the interests of clarity to introduce a distinction at this stage, that between truths and facts. Truths are linguistically stated facts, correct statements, in sum, which, as such, must be formulated in language (broadly understood to include symbols systems of various sorts). A "truth" is something that has to be framed in *linguistic/ symbolic* terms—the representation of a fact through its statement in some language, so that any correct statement represents a truth.

A "fact," on the other hand, is not a linguistic item at all, but an actual aspect of the world's state of affairs which is thereby a feature of reality.[4] Facts correspond to *potential* truths whose actualization as such waits upon their appropriate linguistic embodiment. Truths are statements and thus language-bound, but facts outrun linguistic limits. Once stated, a fact yields a truth, but with facts at large there need in principle be no linguistic route to get from here to there. For one thing, any adequate account of inquiry must recognize that the process of information acquisition at issue in science is a process of *conceptual* innovation. In consequence, the ongoing progress of scientific inquiry always leaves various facts about the things of this world wholly outside the conceptual realm of the inquirers of any particular period. Grasping such a fact means taking a perspective of consideration that as yet we simply do not have, because the state of knowledge (or purported knowledge) has not reached a point at which such a consideration is *feasible*.

And on this basis the facts about any actual physical object are in theory inexhaustible. Its susceptibility to further elaborate detail— and to potential changes of mind regarding this further detail—is built into our very conception of a "real thing." The range of fact about anything real is thus effectively inexhaustible. There is, as best we can tell, no limit to the world's ever-increasing complexity that comes to view with our ever-increasing grasp of its detail. The realm of fact and reality is endlessly variegated and complex. And so we also arrive at:

THESIS 3: THE INEXHAUSTIBILITY OF FACT

Facts are infinite in number. The domain of fact is inexhaustible: there is no limit to facts about the real.

In this regard, however, real things differ in an interesting and important way from fictive ones. For a key about *fictional* particulars is that they are of finite cognitive depth. In characterizing them we shall ultimately run out of steam as regards their nongeneric features. A point will always be reached when one cannot say anything further that is characteristically new about them—presenting nongeneric information that is not inferentially implicit in what has already been said.[5] New *generic* information can, of course, always be forthcoming through the progress of science: when we learn more about coal in general, then we know more about the coal in Sherlock Holmes's grate. But the finiteness of their cognitive depth means that the prospect of ampliatively novel *nongeneric* information must, by the very nature of the case, come to a stop when fictional things are at issue. Something whose character was exhaustible by linguistic characterization would thereby be marked as fictional rather than real.[6]

With *real* things, on the other hand, there is no reason of principle why the elaboration of no generically idiosyncratic information need ever end. On the contrary, we have every reason to presume real things to be cognitively inexhaustible. The prospect of discovery is open-ended here. A recommitment to description-transcending features—no matter how far description is pushed—is essential to our conception of a real thing.

The detail of the real world is inexhaustible: obtaining fuller information about its constituents is always possible in principle—though not of course in practice, since only a finite number of things have actually been said up to now—or indeed up to any actually realized moment of world history. And so we have it that facts regarding reality are infinite in number. But just how infinite?

While our linguistically formulated statements can be enumerated and truths are consequently denumerable in number, there is good reason to suppose that this will not hold for facts. For the reality of it is that facts, unlike truths, cannot be enumerated: *no listing of fact-presenting truths—not even one of infinite length—can possibly manage to constitute a complete register of facts.* Any attempt to register fact as a whole will founder: the list is bound to be incomplete because there are facts about the list as a whole that no single entry can encompass. We thus arrive at yet another salient thesis:

THESIS 4: THE TRANSDENUMERABILITY OF FACTS

The manifold of fact is transdenumerably infinite.

The idea of a complete listing of all the facts is manifestly impracticable. For consider the following statement. *"The list F of stated facts fails to have this statement on it."* But now suppose this statement to be on the list. Then it clearly does not state a fact, so that the list is after all not a list of the facts (contrary to hypothesis). And so it must be left off the list. But then in consequence that list will not be complete, since the statement is true. Facts, that is to say, can never be listed in toto because there will always be further facts—facts about the entire list itself—that a supposedly complete list could not manage to register.

This conclusion can be rendered still more graphic by the following considerations. Suppose that the list F

$$F: f_1, f_2, f_3, \ldots$$

were to constitute a *complete* enumeration of all facts. And now consider the statement

$$Z: \text{the list } F \text{ takes the form } f_1, f_2, f_3, \ldots$$

By hypothesis, this statement will present a fact. So if F is indeed a complete listing of *all* facts, then there will be an integer k such that

$$Z = f_k$$

Accordingly, Z itself will occupy the k-place on the F listing, so that:

f_k = the list L takes the form $f_1, f_2, f_3, \ldots f_k, \ldots$

But this would require f_k to be an expanded version of itself, which is absurd. With the k-th position of the F listing *already* occupied by f_k, we cannot also squeeze that complex f_k-involving thesis into it.

The crux here is simply that any supposedly complete listing of facts

$f_1, f_2, f_3 \ldots$

will itself exhibit, as a whole, certain features that none of its individual members can encompass. Once those individual entries are fixed and the series is defined, there will be further facts about that series as a whole that its members themselves cannot articulate.

In such circumstances, no purportedly comprehensive listing of truths can actually manage to encompass all facts. This transdenumerability of fact means that the domain of reality-characterizing fact inevitably transcends the limits of our capacity to *express* it, and a fortiori those of our capacity to canvas completely. The realm of fact is endlessly complex, detailed, and diversified in its makeup. And the limitedness of our recursively constituted linguistic resources thus means that our characterizations of the real will always fall short.[7] We arrive at the following:

THESIS 5: FACT PREPONDERANCE

There are quantitatively more facts than truths, because the facts are too numerous for enumerability.

Given the nature of the language systems of finite intelligences—and even of finalized symbolic languages—only a denumerable number of statements can ever possibly be made. And yet we know that the number of facts in real-number arithmetic is transdenumerably large. There will thus have to be facts in real-number arithmetic that no one will ever state. It is not that these facts are unstatable in theory, but just that no one will ever state them in practice.

And so, language cannot capture the entirety of fact. It is not only possible but (apparently) likely that we live in a world that is not digital but analog, and whose manifold of states of affairs is simply too rich to be fully comprehended by our linguistically digital means. Truth is to fact what film is to reality—a merely discretized approximation. Cognition, being bound to language, is digital and sequentially linear. Reality, by contrast, is analogue and replete with feedback loops and nonsequentially systemic interrelations. It should thus not be seen as all that surprising that the two cannot be brought into smooth alignment. The comparative limitedness of language-encapsulable truth points to an inevitable limitedness—and thereby incompleteness!—of our knowledge.

First and foremost this means that our knowledge of the world's realities is incomplete—and inevitably so!—because we finite intelligences lack the means for reality's comprehensive characterization. Reality in all its blooming buzzing complexity is too rich for faithful representation by the recursive and enumerable resources of our language. We do and must recognize the limitations of our cognition, acknowledging that we cannot justifiably equate facticity with what can explicitly be known by us through the resources of language. And what transpires here for the circumstantial situation of us humans obtains equally for any other sort of finite intelligence as well. Any physically realizable sort of cognizing being can articulate—and thus can know—only a part or aspect of the real.

Knowing facts is in one respect akin to counting integers—it is something that must be done seriatim: one at a time.[8] And this means, among other things, the following:

1. The manifold at issue being inexhaustible, we can never come to grips with all of its items as particular individuals.

2. Nevertheless, further progress is always possible: in principle we can always go beyond whatever point we have so far managed to reach.

3. Nevertheless, further progress gets ever more cumbersome. In moving onward we must be ever more prolix and make use of ever more elaborate symbol complexes so that greater demands in time, effort, and resources are unavoidable.

4. Accordingly, in actual practice there will be only so much that we can effectively manage to do. The possibilities that obtain in principle can never be fully realized in practice.

5. However, such limitations do not hamper the prospects of establishing various correct generalizations about the manifold in its abstract entirety.

LANGUAGE CANNOT ENCOMPASS FACT: MUSICAL CHAIRS

It is instructive at this point to consider once more the analogy of musical chairs. Of course any individual player can/might be seated. And the same goes for any team or group, with one exception; namely, the whole lot. But since the manifold of knowable truth is denumerable and the manifold of fact in toto is not, then (as in our musical chairs example) the range of the practicable will not, cannot encompass the whole. (And note then that while a team of individuals is not an individual, a complex of facts will nevertheless constitute a fact.)

With regard to language, too, we once again confront a musical chairs situation. Conceivably, language-at-large might, in the abstract, manage to encompass nondenumerably many instances—particularly so if we indulge the prospect of idealization and resort to Bolzano's *Saetze an sich*, Frege's *denkerlose Gedanken*, and the like. But given the granular structure of a universe pervaded by atoms and molecules, only a denumerable number of language-using creatures can ever be squeezed into the fabric of the cosmos. And so the realistically practicable possibilities of *available* languages are at best denumerable.

When reality and language play their game of musical chairs, some facts are bound to be left in the lurch when the music of language stops. The discrepancy manifests itself in the difference between *any* and *every*. Any candidate can possibly be accommodated in seating/stating. (We have $[\forall x]\Diamond[\exists y)]Syx$.) But it is not possible to accommodate every candidate. (We do *not* have $\Diamond[\forall x][\exists y]Syx$.) The limits of knowledge are thus in the final analysis quantitative. The crux of the problem is a discrepancy of numbers. They root in the Musical Chairs Perplex—in the fact that the realm of fact is too vast for the restrictive confines of propositionalized language.

The situation contended here has important cognitive ramifications that are brought to view by the following line of thought:

1. Everything there is—and indeed even presumably everything there possibly can be—has an idiosyncratic property, some feature, no doubt complex and perhaps composite, that holds for it and it alone. (Metaphysical principle)

2. The possession of such a unique characteristic property cannot obtain in virtue of the fact that the item at issue is of a certain natural kind or generic type. It can only obtain in virtue of something appertaining to this item individually and specifically.

3. Accordingly, for anything whatsoever, there is a fact—namely, that that thing has that particular idiosyncratic property—that you can know only if you can individuate and specify that particular thing.

4. The inherent limitations of language mean that there are more things that it is possible to individuate and specify.

The inevitability of unknown facts emerges at once from these considerations of general principle.

The reality of it is that the domain of fact is ampler than that of truth, so that language cannot capture the entirety of fact. We live in a world that is not digital but analog, and so the manifold of its states of affairs is simply too rich to be fully comprehended by our linguistically digital means.[9] The domain of fact inevitably transcends the limits of our capacity to *express* it, and a fortiori those of our capacity to canvass it in overt detail. Truth is to fact what moving pictures are to reality—a merely discretized approximation.

To be sure, the numerical discrepancy at issue with the Musical Chairs Perplex does no more than establish the existence of *unknown* facts. It does not get so far as to establish the existence of facts that are inherently *unknowable*, facts which cannot, as a matter of principle, possibly be known. To see what can be done in this direction, we shall have to look at matters in a different light.

There clearly is, however, one fact that is unstatable to language and thereby unknowable by creatures whose knowledge is confined to the linguistically formulatable. This is the grand mega-fact consisting of the amalgamation of all facts whatever. For language-dependent knowers can at most and at best have cognitive access to a denumerable number of facts, whereas factuality itself in principle encompasses a nondenumerable quantity.

And an important point is at issue here. With musical chairs we know that there will be someone unseated, but cannot (given the ordinary contingencies) manage to say *who* this will be. And with facts, which from a cognitive point of view reduplicate the musical chairs situation, we also cannot manage to say which facts will be unknown. For here, too, there is a room for contingency. But there is one very big difference. With musical chairs the totality of individuals, while of course not sealable, does not combine to form a single unseatable mega-individual. But the totality of facts—which cannot possibly be known—does arguably combine to form one grand unknowable megafact—the Reality of things, if you will.

Be this as it may, one crucial consideration stands before us. The quantitative disparity between truth and fact means that there is inevitably going to be a vast amount of fact about reality of which we are going to be ignorant.[10]

Cognitive Finitude

First the good news. Generalizations can of course refer to *every-thing*. Bishop Butler's "Everything is what it is and not another thing" holds with unrestricted universality. And once continuous quantities are introduced, the range of *inferentially available* statements becomes uncountable. "The length of the table exceeds x inches." Once known, this straightaway opens the door to uncountable knowable consequences. And fortunately, a case-by-case determination is not generally needed to validate generalizations. We can establish claims about groups larger than we can ever hope to inventory. Recourse to arbitrary instances, the process of indirect proof by reductio ad absurdum, and induction (mathematical and scientific) all afford procedures for achieving generality knowledge beyond the reach of an exhaustive case-by-case check.

But will this *always* be so? Or are there also general truths whose determination would require the exhaustive surveying of all specific instances of a totality too large for our range of vision? At this point our cognitive finitude becomes a crucial consideration, and the difference between finite and infinite knowers becomes of fundamental importance and requires closer elucidation. For an infinite knower need not and should not be construed as an *omniscient* knower—one from whom nothing knowable is concealed (and so who knows, for example, who will be elected U.S. president in the year 2200). Rather, what is at issue is a knower who can manage to know in individualized detail an infinite number of independent facts. (Such a knower might, for example, be able to answer such a question as, "Will the decimal expansion of π always continue to agree at some future point with that of $\sqrt{2}$ for 100 decimal places?") Finite knowers cannot manage this sort of thing.

Finite knowers can, of course, know universal truths. After all, we must acknowledge the prospect of inductive knowledge of general laws, and we will have it that a knower can unproblematically know—for example—that "All dogs eat meat."[1] But what finite knowers *cannot* manage is to know this sort of thing *in detail* rather than at the level of generality. They cannot know specifically of each and every u in that potentially infinite range that F_u obtains—that is, while they can know collectively *that all individuals have F*, they cannot know distributively *of every individual that it has F*—something they could not do without knowing who they individually are.

So the issue now before us is that of the question of general truths that can be known *only* by assessing the situation of an intractable manifold of individual cases.

QUASI-QUANTITIES

It is instructive to survey some situations in which the ways of the world impel ignorance upon us. One instance is afforded by quasi-quantities that cannot be pinned down exactly. What is at issue here is a quantity that resists being specified precisely by a particular number. It admits of being located within a certain numerical range while nevertheless not letting itself be made precise. It is, in sum, a quantity X such that for any real number n the claim $X = n$ is untenable, and not just false but even meaningless or silly, even though $n_1 < X < n_2$ may well be true. So when X is a quasi-quantity in the aforementioned sense, then there will be some values of u so small that X specifying X to within a limit of size u is no longer meaningful. With a quasi-quantity we cannot be exact beyond a certain point (a point about which itself we cannot be absolutely exact).

The weight of a person is just like that. Just how much air is in his lungs at the moment? Does that hair or that flake of skin just now detaching from him count or not count? What about that drop of perspiration just dropping off his nose? We can meaningfully specify weight to within the nearest X for X down to perhaps a milligram, but we cannot push the matter far below that.

Much the same goes for a person's age, seeing that the moment of someone's birth can be pinned down only so far. And of course the current length of Britain's coastline can only be managed to within rough limits, what with tides and waves and such.

An interesting question arises in this connection. Are there any situations in life (or, indeed, even in science) where *extreme* precision actually matters, where the fact that X is a quasi-quantity rather than a precise quantity makes a difference to anything—and "being as precise as one can reasonably be expected to be in matters of this kind" is not good enough?

There will indeed be, specifically in those situations that physicists characterize as chaotic. In these instances, there will be quantities that operate in the context of functional relationships, where a difference in input, however minute, will always make a substantive difference in output. Hence the outcome depends on matters that ultimately are wholly below and beyond the threshold of our vision. The precision needed to go from speculation to calculation is simply beyond our reach in such cases. As far as we are concerned, the matter will be a thing of pure chance. We cannot effectively come to know the details of it. In drastic matters, quasi-quantities will impel us into ignorance

SURD FEATURES

There are two sorts of properties of objects: namely *generic* properties that an object shares with all others of a particular natural kind to which it belongs, and idiosyncratic properties that characterize it uniquely without in anyway inhering in a natural kind to which it belongs. An object's possession of such idiosyncratic properties cannot be derived from laws that are given its constitution in terms of general kinds. They cannot be determined by descriptions but require individual, specific inspection.

Thus, if each individual of an infinite set has an idiosyncratic property, then no finite intelligence can ever know this array of fact in detail. (In the end this is bound to be the case with the positive integers, for example.) One cannot, of course, provide concrete examples of facts that are unknowable to finite knowers, seeing that a claim to factuality automatically carries a claim to knowledge in its wake. However, while we cannot know specifically *which* is such a fact, one can certainly substantiate the claim generally *that* there are such things. Let us consider this situation more closely.

A feature F of an object/item x is *surd* if Fx cannot be deduced from the body of knowledge consisting of the following:

- The identifying (discussion-introducing) descriptive characterization of the item x at issue

- A specification of the various natural kinds (K_i) to which said item x belongs, together with
- A specification of the various kind-correlative laws— all given by generalizations having the structure: "Everything of kind K has the property F"

A second feature of an item is, in sum, one that cannot be established from general principles after that item has been duly identified. Such a feature is idiosyncratic to that item in conditions taken to all others of its kind with respect to each and every one of its several kinds to which it belongs.

For example, it is *not* the case that "being a prime" is a surd property of 5. For the nondivisibility of 5 by any lesser integer (save 1) can be deduced from 5's defining specification, together with the general laws of arithmetic that govern integers at large (a natural kind of which 5 belongs). By contrast, "being the number of books on that table" is a surd property of 5, seeing that there is no way of deriving it from the general principles at issue with the characterizing specification of 5, together with the laws that govern its correlative natural kinds.

Accordingly, the specifically *surd* feature of objects/items are those facts about them that are not inferentially accessible from a knowledge of their nature—and thereby not explicable through recourse to general principles. As far as the relevant corpus of general principles is concerned, the feature is anomalous, contingent, and is by its very nature not law-rationalizable.[2] Its possession by an object has to be determined by inspection: it cannot be established by inference from that object's specifying features via general principles.

Given this understanding of the matter, let us suppose that some mind feature or other stands in common by each and every member of some infinite or open-ended set of terms. Since this fact cannot (ex hypothesi) be established on general principles, it will have to be revised through case-by-case inspection, which—in these circumstances—is unpreventable with any finite knower.

For example, it must be granted that as long as these astronomical objects persist there will, on any given day, be a number of meteors (with mass greater than 1 kg) closer to the earth than to the moon. And now consider the contention that this number is invariably less than five thousand. It may well be that this contention is true. But since the number of relevant days is—potentially—infinitely large and since the matter is not one that can be settled for each of these several days on the basis of general automated principles, the fact now hypothetically at issue (namely, that the number in question is never greater than five thousand) is something that finite intelligence cannot possibly come to know.

And this illustrates the fact that *finite knowers can never ascertain the surd/contingent general features of an infinite or indefinitely large collection.* For our knowledge of the universal features of infinite groups is limited to the reach of lawful generalizations alone. Determination of surd generality would require an item-by-item check, which is by hypothesis impracticable for us with infinite or indefinite collections. Accordingly, where such large groups are concerned, secure general knowledge is confined to the region of nomic fact. Though there will doubtless be universal facts that are surd in character in our complex world, they remain, for us, in the realm of supposition and conjecture. For finite knowers, firm knowledge of surd universality is unrealizable.

Such examples illustrate the general phenomenon that finite knowers can never decisively establish a surd/contingent general feature of an infinitely or indefinitely large collection. For whenever a generality holds for a collection on a merely contingent basis, this is something that we finite intelligences can never determine with categorical assurance, because determination of such kind-pervasive surdity would require an item-by-item check, which is by hypothesis impracticable for us. This situation clearly manifests yet another sort of inevitable ignorance in finite intelligences.

THE PRINCIPLE OF EPISTEMIC DISPARITY

Let us begin here with a somewhat extreme case. A knower is *unrestrictedly* omniscient. Whenever there is something to be known, this knower knows it. In other words, whenever *p* is a true matter of fact, the knower knows that it is so. Thus, *x* is omniscient in this sense if we have:

$$(\forall p)(p \rightarrow Kxp)$$

Such a knower knows everything that is knowable. This knower's knowledge is literally unlimited: something is a truth if, and only if, our omniscient being *x* knows it.

By contrast, a knower is *restrictedly* omniscient iff this knower knows everything that is known. That is, whenever *anyone* knows something, this knower knows it as well: Thus *x* is omniscient in this weaker sense if we have:

$$(\forall p)(\exists y Kyp \rightarrow Kxp)$$

The difference between the two modes of omniscience can come into operation only when there are unknowns—that is, truths which nobody knows at all. For when we have

$$p \ \& \sim (\exists y)Kxp$$

the antecedent at issue with unrestricted omniscience is satisfied, while that at issue with restricted omniscience is not.

How do I know that I am not omniscient? Certainly not because I can specify particular facts that I do not know. Rather, it is because there are questions I cannot answer—and because I realize full well at the level of generality that there are truth-determinate propositions whose truth-status I cannot decide, perfectly meaningful propositions about authentic matters of fact that I know neither to be true nor false, even though I do know that they have to be one or the other. (That George Washington wondered if Martha was suitably dressed for the occasion of his first inauguration would seem to be a good example.) But what of others?

There can be no doubt that ignorance exacts its price in incomprehension. And here it helps to consider the matter in a somewhat theological light. The world we live in is a manifold that is not of our making but of Reality's—or of God's, if you will. And what is now at issue might be called Isaiah's Principle on the basis of the following verse:

> For My thoughts are not your thoughts, neither are your
> ways My way, says the LORD. For as the heavens are
> higher than the Earth, so are My ways higher than your
> ways, and My thoughts than your thoughts. (Isa. 55:8–9)

A fundamental law of epistemology is at work here—to wit, the principle that *a mind of lesser power is for this very reason unable to understand adequately the workings of a mind of greater power.* To be sure, the weaker mind can doubtless realize *that* the stronger can solve problems it itself cannot. But it cannot understand *how* it is able to do so. An intellect that can only just manage to do well at tic-tac-toe cannot possibly comprehend the ways of one that is expert at chess.

The knowledge of limited knowers is inevitably limited in point of detail. The lesser mind can know *that* the more powerful has certain things but cannot tell the *what* and the *how* of it. To the lesser mind, the performances of a more powerful one are bound to seem like magic.

Consider in this light the vast disparity of computational power between a mathematical tyro like most of us and a mathematical prodigy like Ramanujan. Not only cannot our tyro manage to answer the number-theoretic question that such a genius resolves in the blink of an eye, but the tyro cannot even begin to understand the processes and procedures that the Indian genius employs. As far as the tyro is concerned, it is all sheer wizardry. No doubt once an answer is given, he can check its correctness. But actually finding the answer is something that lesser intellect cannot manage—the how of the business lies beyond its grasp. And, for much the same sort of reason, a mind of lesser power cannot discover what the question-resolving limits of a mind of greater power are. It can never say with warranted assurance where the limits of question-resolving power lie. (In some instances it may be able to say what's in and what's out, but never map the dividing boundary.)

The Old Testament is strikingly explicit on these matters: "Who has understood the mind of the LORD, or instructed him as his counselor? Whom did the LORD consult to enlighten him, and who taught him the right way? Who was it that taught him knowledge or showed him the path of understanding?" (Isa. 40:13–14). And Christian theologians proceed along the same line, as per the teachings of St. Thomas Aquinas: "The knowledge that is natural to us has its source in our senses and therefore extends just as far as it can be led by sensible things. But our understanding cannot reach to an apprehension of God's essence from these."[3] It is not simply that a more powerful mind will know quantitatively more facts than a less powerful one, but that its conceptual machinery is ampler in encompassing ideas and issues that are quantitatively inaccessible in lying altogether outside the conceptual horizon of its less powerful compeers.

Now insofar as the relation of a lesser toward a higher intelligence is substantially analogous to the relation between an earlier state of science and a later state, some instructive lessons emerge. It is not that Aristotle could not have comprehended quantum theory—he was a very smart fellow and could certainly have learned. But he could not have formulated quantum theory within his own conceptual framework, his own familiar terms of reference. The very ideas at issue lay outside of the conceptual horizon of Aristotle's science, and, like present-day students, he would have had to master them from the ground up. Just this sort of thing is at issue with the relation of a less powerful intelligence to a more powerful one. It has been said insightfully that from the vantage point of a less developed technology, another, substantially advanced technology is indistinguishable from magic. And exactly the same holds for a more advanced *conceptual* (rather than physical) technology.

It is instructive to contemplate in this light the hopeless difficulties that nowadays confront the popularization of physics—of trying to characterize the implications of quantum theory and relativity theory for cosmology into the subscientific language of everyday life. A classic *obiter dictum* of Niels Bohr is relevant: "We must be clear that, when it comes to atoms, language can be used only as in poetry." If the thought that is conceptualized in the operations of physical reality is, so to speak, reflective of the work of a mind more powerful than ours, then an adequate apprehension of nature will prove beyond our grasp, so that here too an unavoidable ignorance falls to our lot.

On Limits to Science

CONDITIONS OF PERFECTED SCIENCE

One sagacious commentator wrote that "the sudden confrontation with the depth and scope of our ignorance represents the most significant contribution of twentieth-century science to the human intellect."[1] But are there matters regarding nature about which we will *remain* ignorant? How far can the scientific enterprise advance toward a definitive understanding of reality? Might science attain a point of recognizable completion? Is the achievement of perfected science a genuine possibility, even in theory, when all of the "merely practical" obstacles are put aside as somehow incidental?

What would *perfected* or *completed* science be like? What sort of standards would it have to meet? Clearly, it would have to complete in full the discharge of natural science's mandate or mission. And the goal-structure of scientific inquiry covers a good deal of diversified and complex ground, encompassing the traditional quartet of description, explanation, prediction, and control, in line with display 5.1.

Display 5.1. The aims of science

theoretical goals	DESCRIPTION (answering *what* and *how* questions about nature)	cognitive goals
	EXPLANATION (answering *why* questions about nature)	
practical goals	PREDICTION (successful alignment of our expectations regarding nature)	manipulative goals
	CONTROL (effective intervention in nature to alter the course of events in desired directions)	

In short, the theoretical sector concerns itself with matters of characterizing, explaining, accounting for, and rendering intelligible—with purely intellectual and informative issues. By contrast, the practical sector is concerned with guiding actions, canalizing expectations, and, in general, achieving the control over our environment that is required for the satisfactory conduct of our affairs. The former sector thus deals with what science enables us to *say*, and the latter with what it enables us to *do*. The one relates to our role as spectators of nature, the other to our role as active participants.

It thus appears that if we are to claim that our science has attained a perfected condition, it would have to satisfy (at least) the four following conditions:

1. Erotetic completeness: It must answer, in principle at any rate, all those descriptive and explanatory questions that it itself countenances as legitimately raisable, and must accordingly explain everything it deems explicable.

2. Predictive completeness: It must provide the cognitive basis for accurately predicting those eventuations that

are in principle predictable (that is, those which it itself recognizes as such).

3. Pragmatic completeness: It must provide the requisite cognitive means for doing whatever is feasible for beings like ourselves to do in the circumstances in which we labor.

4. Temporal finality (the omega-condition): It must leave no room for expecting further substantial changes that destabilize the existing state of scientific knowledge.

Each of these modes of substantive completeness deserves detailed consideration.

THEORETICAL ADEQUACY: ISSUES OF EROTETIC COMPLETENESS

It is clear that the question

What's an example of a truth one cannot establish as such—a fact that we cannot come to know?

is one that leads ad absurdum. The quest for unknowable facts is inherently quixotic and paradoxical because of the inherent conflict between the definitive features at issue—factuality and unknowability. Here we must abandon the demand for *knowledge* and settle for mere *conjecture*. But how far can we go in this direction?

Clearly there are obstacles here, posed by questions that cannot be answered satisfactorily one way or another because every possible answer is unavailable on grounds of *an evidential insufficiency of accessible information*.

Consider some possible examples of this phenomenon. In 1880 the German physiologist, philosopher, and historian of science Emil du Bois-Reymond published a widely discussed lecture of *The Seven Riddles of the Universe* (Die sieben Welträtsel), in which he maintained that some of the most fundamental problems regarding the workings of the world were irresolvable. Du Bois-Reymond was a rigorous mechanist. In his view, nonmechanical modes of inquiry cannot produce adequate results, and the limit of our secure knowledge of the world is confined to the range where purely mechanical principles can be applied. As for all else, we not only *do not* have but *cannot* in principle obtain reliable knowledge. Under the banner of the slogan *"ignoramus et ignorabimus"* (we *do not* know and *shall never* know), du Bois-Reymond maintained a sceptically agnostic position with respect to basic issues in physics (the nature of matter and of force, and the ultimate source of motion) and psychology (the origin of sensation and of consciousness). These issues are simply *insolubilia* which transcend man's scientific capabilities. Certain fundamental biological problems he regarded as unsolved but perhaps in principle soluble (though very difficult): the origin of life, the adaptiveness of organisms, and the development of language and reason. Regarding the seventh riddle—the problem of freedom of the will—he was undecided.

The position of du Bois-Reymond was swiftly and sharply contested by the zoologist Ernest Haeckel in *Die Welträtsel,* published in 1889, which soon attained a great popularity. Far from being intractable or even insoluble—so Haeckel maintained—the riddles of du Bois-Reymond had all virtually been solved. Dismissing the problem of free will as a pseudo-problem—since free will "is a pure dogma [which] rests on mere illusion and in reality does not exist at all"—Haeckel turned with relish to the remaining riddles. Problems of the origin of life, of sensation, and of consciousness Haeckel regarded as solved—or solvable—by appeal to the theory of evolution. Questions of the nature of matter and force he regarded as solved by modern physics, except for one: the problem (perhaps less scientific than metaphysical) of the ultimate origin of matter and its laws. This "problem of substance" was the only remaining riddle recognized by Haeckel, and it was not really a problem of science: in discovering the "fundamental law of the conservation of matter and force," science had done pretty much what it could do with respect to this problem—the rest that remained was metaphysics, with which the scientist had no proper concern. Haeckel summarized his position as follows:

> The number of world-riddles has been continually diminishing in the course of the nineteenth century through the aforesaid progress of a true knowledge of nature. Only one comprehensive riddle of the universe now remains—the problem of substance. . . . [But now] we have the great, comprehensive "law of substance," the fundamental law of the constancy of matter and force. The fact that substance is everywhere subject to eternal movement and transformation gives it the character also of the universal law of evolution. As this supreme law has been firmly established, and all others are subordinate to it, we arrive at a conviction of the universal unity of nature and the eternal validity of its laws. From the gloomy *problem* of substance we have evolved the clear *law* of substance.

And in this spirit the English theoretician Karl Pearson wrote:

> Now I venture to think that there is great danger in this cry, "We *shall* be ignorant." To cry "We are ignorant" is sage and healthy, but the attempt to demonstrate an endless futurity of ignorance appears a modesty which approaches despair. Conscious of the past great achievements and the present restless activity of science, may we not do better to accept as our watchword that challenge of Galilei: "Who is willing to set limits to the human intellect?"—reinterpreting it by what evolution has

taught us of the continual growth of man's intellectual powers.[2]

The basic structure of Haeckel's position is clear: science is rapidly nearing a state where all the big problems have been solved. What remains unresolved is not so much a *scientific* as a *metaphysical* problem. In science itself, the big battle is virtually at an end, and the work that remains is pretty much mopping-up operations.

But is this rather optimistic position tenable? Can we really dismiss the prospect of factual insolubilia? Observe, to begin with, that even if one were to agree with C. S. Peirce that science is en route to a completion, we may well always—at *any* given time—remain at a remove from ultimacy. For as long as the body of knowledge continues to grow, there will still remain scope for the possibility of insolubilia. Even an asymptotically complete-able science can accommodate a fixed region of unresolvability, as long as the scope of that science itself is growing. That is, even if the *fraction* of unresolved questions converges asymptotically to zero, the *number* of unresolved questions may be ever growing in the context of an expanding science. For consider the following:

Number of questions on the agenda	100	1000	10,000	10^k
Fraction of unresolved questions	$\frac{1}{2}$	$\frac{1}{4}$	$\frac{1}{8}$	$(\frac{1}{2})^{k-1}$
Number of unresolved questions	50	250	1250	$10^k \times (\frac{1}{2})^{k-1}$

As these figures indicate, there is room for insolubilia even within a science ever improving so as to approach asymptotic completeness. And this points toward a prospect that is well worth exploring.

But could we ever actually achieve erotetic completeness (*Q*-completeness)—the condition of being able to resolve, in principle, all of our (legitimately posable) questions about the world? Could we ever find ourselves in this position?[3] Prescinding, for the moment, from Kant's Principle of Question proliferation, it could be supposed that a body of science could be such as to provide answers to all of the questions that it allows to arise. But just how meaningful would this mode of completeness be?

It is sobering to realize that the erotetic completeness of a stage of science does not necessarily betoken its comprehensiveness or sufficiency. For it might reflect the paucity of the range of questions we are prepared to contemplate—a deficiency of imagination, so to speak. When the range of our knowledge is sufficiently restricted, then its question-resolving completeness could merely reflect this impoverishment rather than its intrinsic adequacy. Conceivably, if improbably, science might reach a purely fortuitous equilibrium between problems and solutions through being "completed" in the narrow erotetic sense of providing an answer to every question in the then-existing (albeit still imperfect) state of knowledge. And so our corpus of scientific knowledge could be erotetically complete and yet fundamentally inadequate.

THE INACCESSIBILITY OF FUTURE SCIENCE

The reality of it is that any adequate theory of inquiry must recognize that the ongoing process of science is a process of *conceptual* innovation that always leaves certain theses wholly outside the cognitive range of the inquirers of any particular period. Having never contemplated electronic computing machines as such, the ancient Romans could also venture no predictions about their impact on the social and economic life of the twenty-first century. Clever though he unquestionably was, Aristotle could not have pondered the issues of quantum electrodynamics. The scientific questions of the future are—at least in part—bound to be conceptually inaccessible to the inquirers of the present. The question of just how the cognitive agenda of some future date will be constituted is clearly irresolvable for us now. Not only can we not anticipate future discoveries now; we cannot even prediscern the questions that will arise as time moves on, and cognitive progress with it.[4] We are cognitively myopic with respect to future knowledge. It is in principle infeasible for us to say now what questions will figure in the erotetic agenda of the future, let alone what answers they will engender. And this means that there will always be facts (or plausible candidate facts) about a thing that we do not *know* because we cannot even conceive of them. For to grasp such facts calls for taking a perspective of consideration that we simply do not have, since the state of knowledge (or purported knowledge) is not yet advanced to a point at which its entertainment is feasible. In bringing conceptual innovation about, cognitive progress makes it possible to consider new possibilities that were heretofore conceptually inaccessible.

We may be able to discover or surmise what questions someone will be able to answer in the future on the basis of new discoveries. But we will, of course, have no choice as to what those answers will be. The language of emergence can perhaps be deployed profitably to make the point. However, what is at issue is not an emergence of *the features of things* but an emergence in our *knowledge* about them. The blood circulated in the human body well before Harvey; uranium-containing substances were radioactive before Becquerel. The emergence at issue relates to our cognitive mechanisms of conceptualization, not to the objects of our consideration in and of themselves. Real-world objects are conceived of as antecedent to any cognitive interaction—as being there right along, or "pregiven," as Edmund Husserl puts it. Any cognitive changes or innovations are to be conceptualized as something that occurs on our side of the cognitive transaction, not on the side of the objects with which we deal.[5]

The prospect of change can never be dismissed in this domain. The properties of a thing are literally open-ended: we can always discover more of them. Even if one were to view the world as inherently finite and espouse a Principle of Limited Variety, which has it that nature can be portrayed descriptively with the materials of a finite taxonomic scheme, there can be no a priori guarantee that the progress of science will not engender an unending sequence of changes of mind regarding the constitution of this finite register of descriptive materials. And this conforms exactly to our expectation in these matters. For where the real things of the world are concerned, we not only expect to learn more about them in the course of scientific inquiry, *we expect to have to change our mind about their nature and mode of comportment.* Be it elm trees, volcanoes, or quarks that are at issue, we have every expectation that in the course of future scientific progress people will come to think differently about them than we do.

Cognitive inexhaustibility is in fact a definitive feature of our conception of a real thing. For in claiming knowledge about them we are always aware that the actual features of any object will always transcend what we know about it—that yet further and different facts concerning it can always come to light, and that all that we *do* say about it does not exhaust all that *can* be said about it.

The preceding considerations illustrate a more general circumstance. Any claim to the realization of a *theoretically* complete science of physics would be one that affords "a complete, consistent, and unified theory of physical interaction that would describe all possible observations."[6] But to check that the state of physics on hand actually meets this condition, we would need to know exactly what physical interactions are indeed *possible.* And to warrant us in using the state of physics on hand as a basis for answering *this* question, we would *already* have to be assured that its view of the possibilities is correct—and thus already have preestablished its completeness. The idea of a consolidated erotetic completeness shipwrecks on the infeasibility of finding a meaningful way to monitor its attainment.

This process of judging the adequacy of our science on its own telling is the best we can do, but it remains an essentially circular and consequently inconclusive way of proceeding. The long and short of it is that there is no cognitively adequate basis for maintaining the completeness of science in a rationally satisfactory way.

To monitor the theoretical completeness of science, we require some theory-external control on the adequacy of our theorizing, some theory-external reality principle to serve as a standard of adequacy. We are thus driven to abandoning the road of pure theory and proceeding along that of the practical goals of the enterprise. This gives special importance and urgency to the pragmatic sector.

PRAGMATIC COMPLETENESS

The arbitrament of praxis—not theoretical merit but practical capability—affords the best standard of adequacy for our scientific proceedings that is available. But could we ever be in a position to claim that science has been completed on the basis of the success of its practical applications? On this basis, the perfection of science would have to manifest itself in the perfecting of control—in achieving a perfected technology. But just how are we to proceed here? Could our natural science achieve manifest perfection on the side of control over nature? Could it ever underwrite a recognizably perfected technology?

The issue of control over nature involves much more complexity than may appear on first view. For just how is this conception to be understood? Clearly, in terms of bending the course of events to our will, of attaining our ends within nature. But this involvement of *our ends* brings to light the prominence of our own contribution. For example, if we are inordinately modest in our demands (or very unimaginative), we may even achieve complete control over nature in the sense of being in a position to do *whatever we want* to do, but yet attain this happy condition in a way that betokens very little real capability.

One might, to be sure, involve the idea of omnipotence and construe a "perfected" technology as one that would enable us to do literally *anything*. But this approach would at once run into the old difficulties already familiar to the medieval scholastics. They were faced with the challenge: If God is omnipotent, can he annihilate himself (contra his nature as a *necessary* being), or can he do evil deeds (contra his nature as a *perfect* being), or can he make triangles have four angles (contrary to *their* definitive nature)? Sensibly enough, the scholastics inclined to solve these difficulties by maintaining that an omnipotent God need not be in a position to do literally anything, but rather simply anything that it *is possible* for him to do. Similarly, we cannot explicate the idea of technological omnipotence in terms of a capacity to produce and result, wholly without qualification. We cannot ask for the production of a *perpetuum mobile*, for spaceships with "hyperdrive" enabling them to attain transluminar velocities, for devices that predict essentially stochastic processes such as the disintegrations of transuranic atoms, or for piston devices that enable us to set *independently* the values for the pressure, temperature, and volume of a body of gas. We cannot, in sum, ask of a "perfected" technology that it should enable us to do anything that we might take it into our heads to do.

All that we can reasonably ask of it is that perfected technology should enable us to do anything *that it is possible for us to do*—and not just what we might *think* we can do, but what we really and truly can do. A perfected technology would be one that enables us to do anything that *can possibly* be done by creatures circumstanced as we are. But how can we deal with the pivotal conception of "can" that is at issue here? Clearly, only science—real, true, correct, and in sum *perfected* science—could tell us what in fact is realistically possible and what circumstances are indeed inescapable. Whenever our "knowledge" falls short of this, we may well "ask the impossible" by way of accomplishment (for example, spaceships in "hyperdrive") and thus complain of incapacity to achieve control in ways that put unfair burdens on this conception.

Power is a matter of the effecting of things possible—of achieving control—and it is clearly cognitive state-of-the-art in science, which, in teaching us about the limits of the possible, is itself the agent that must shape our conception of this issue. *Every* law of nature serves to set the boundary between what is genuinely possible and what is not, between what can be done and what cannot, between which questions we can properly ask and which we cannot. We cannot satisfactorily monitor the adequacy and completeness of our science by its ability to effect all things possible, because science alone can inform us about what is possible. As science grows and develops, it poses new issues of power and control, reformulating and reshaping those demands whose realization represents control over nature. For science itself brings new possibilities to light. (At a suitable stage, the idea of splitting the atom will no longer seem a contradiction in terms.) To see if a given state of technology meets the condition of perfection, we must *already* have a body of perfected science in hand to tell us what is indeed possible. To validate the claim that our technology is perfected, we need to *preestablish* the completeness of our science. The idea works in such a way that claims to perfected control can rest only on perfected science.

In attempting to travel the practical route to cognitive completeness, we are thus trapped in a vitiating circle. Short of having supposedly perfected science in hand, we could not say what a perfected technology would be like, and thus we could not possibly monitor the perfection of science in terms of the technology that it underwrites.

Moreover, even if (*per impossible*) a "pragmatic equilibrium" between what we can and what we wish to do in science were to be realized, we could not be warrantedly confident that this condition will remain unchanged. The possibility that "just around the corner things will become unstuck" can never be eliminated. Even if we achieve control, for all intents and purposes, we cannot be sure of not losing our grip upon it—not because of a loss of power but because of cognitive changes that produce a broadening of the imagination and a widened apprehension as to what having control involves.

Accordingly, the project of achieving practical mastery can never be perfected in a satisfactory way. The point is that control hinges on what we want, and what we want is conditioned by what we think possible, and *this* is something that hinges crucially on theory—on our beliefs about how things work in this world. And so control is something deeply theory-infected. We can never safely move from apparent to real adequacy in this regard. We cannot adequately assure that seeming perfection is more than just that. We thus have no alternative but to *presume* that our knowledge (that is, our purported knowledge) is inadequate at this, and indeed at any other particular stage of the game of cognitive completeness.

One important point about control must, however, be noted. Our preceding negative strictures all relate to attainment of perfect control—of being in a position to do everything possible. But no such problems affect the issue of amelioration—of doing some things better and *improving* our control over what it was. It makes perfectly good sense to use its technological applications as standards of scientific advancement. (Indeed, we have no real alternative to using pragmatic standards at this level, because reliance on theory alone is, in the end, going to be circular.) While control does not help us with *perfection*, it is crucial for monitoring *progress*. Standards of assessment and evaluation are such that we can implement the idea of improvements (progress), but not that of completion (realized perfection). We can determine when we have managed to *enlarge* our technological mastery, but we cannot meaningfully say what it would be to *perfect* it. (Our conception of the *doable* keeps changing with changes in the cognitive state-of-the-art, a fact that does not, of course, alter our view of what *already has been done* in the practical sphere.)

With regard to technical perfectibility, we must recognize that (1) there is no reason to expect that its realization is possible, even in principle, and (2) it cannot be monitored: even if we had achieved it, we would not be able to claim success with warranted confidence. In the final analysis, then, we cannot regard the *realization* of "completed science" as a meaningful prospect—we cannot really say what it is that we are asking for. (To be sure, what is meaningless here is not the idea of perfected science as such but the idea of *achieving* it.) These deliberations further substantiate the idea that we must always presume our knowledge to be incomplete in the domain of natural science.

PREDICTIVE COMPLETENESS

Predictive completeness rests on the idea of being able to predict everything that occurs. It represents a forlorn hope. For predictors are—of necessity!—bound to fail even in much simpler self-predictive matters. Thus consider confronting a predictor with the problem posed by the following question:

P_1: *When next you answer a question, will the answer be negative?*

This is a question which—for reasons of general principle—no predictor can ever answer satisfactorily.[7] For consider the available possibilities:

Answer given	Agreement?	Actually correct answer?
Yes	No	No
No	Yes	No
Can't say	No	No

On this question, there just is no way in which a predictor's response could possibly agree with the actual fact of the matter. Even the seemingly plausible response of "I can't say" automatically constitutes a self-falsifying answer, since in giving this answer the predictor would automatically make "No" into the response called for by the proprieties of the situation.

Of course the problem poses a perfectly meaningful question to which *another* predictor could give a putatively correct answer— namely, by saying, "No—that predictor cannot answer this question at all; the question will condemn a predictor to baffled silence." However, while the question posed in P_1 will be irresolvable by a *particular* computer, it could—in theory—be answered by *other* predictors and so is not flat-out predictively intractable. But there are other questions that indeed are computer insolubilia for computers-at-large. One of them is the following:

P_2: *What is an example of a predictive question that no*
        predictor will ever state?

In answering *this* question the predictor would have to stake a claim of the form: "Q is an example of a predictive question that no predictor will ever state." And in the very making of this claim the predictor would falsify it. It is thus automatically unable to effect a satisfactory resolution. However, the question is neither meaningless nor irresolvable. A *noncomputer* problem solver could in theory answer it correctly. All the same, its presupposition, "There is a predictive question that no predictor will ever consider" is beyond doubt true.

What we thus have in P_2 is an example of an in-principle solvable—and thus "meaningful"—question that, as a matter of necessity in the logical scheme of things, no predictor can ever resolve satisfactorily.

The difficulties encountered in using physical control as a standard of "perfection" in science all also hold with respect to *prediction*, which, after all, is simply a mode of *cognitive* control.

One of the prime obstacles to the predictive incompleteness of science relates to the issue of science itself. In scientific inquiry as in other sectors of human affairs, major upheavals can come about in a manner that is sudden, unanticipated, and often unwelcome. Major breakthroughs often result from research projects that have very different ends in view. Louis Pasteur's discovery of the protective efficacy of inoculation with weakened disease strains affords a striking example. While studying chicken cholera, Pasteur accidentally inoculated a group of chickens with a weak culture. The chickens became ill, but, instead of dying, recovered. Pasteur later reinoculated these chickens with fresh culture—one strong enough to kill an ordinary chicken. To Pasteur's surprise, the chickens remained healthy. Pasteur then shifted his attention to this interesting phenomenon, and a productive new line of investigation opened up. In empirical inquiry, we generally cannot tell in advance what further questions will be engendered by our endeavors to answer those on hand, those answers themselves being as yet unavailable. Accordingly, the issues of future science simply lie beyond our present horizons.

The past may be a different country, but the future is a terra incognita. Its entire cognitive landscape—its science, its technology, its intellectual fads and fashions, etc.—all lie outside our ken. We cannot begin to say what ideas will be at work here, though we know on general principles they will differ from our own. And whenever our ideas cannot penetrate, we are for that very reason impotent to make any detailed predictions.

Throughout the domain of inventive production in science, technology, and the arts we find processes of creative innovation whose features defy all prospects of predictability. We know—or at any rate can safely predict—*that* future science will make major discoveries (both theoretical and observational/phenomenological) in the next century, but we cannot say *what* they are and *how* they will be made (since otherwise we could proceed to make them here and now).[8] We could not possibly predict now the substantive content of our future discoveries—those that result from our future cognitive choices—because that would transform them into present discoveries, which, by hypothesis, they are not. In the context of questions about matters of scientific importance, then, we must be prepared for surprises.

It is a key fact of life that ongoing progress in scientific inquiry is a process of *conceptual* innovation that always places certain developments outside the cognitive horizons of earlier workers because the very concepts operative in their characterization become available only in the course of scientific discovery itself. (Short of learning our science from the ground up, Aristotle could have made nothing of modern genetics.) Newton could not have predicted findings in quantum theory any more than he could have predicted the outcome of American presidential elections. We cannot now predict the future states of scientific knowledge in detail because we do not yet have at our disposal the very concepts in which the issues will be posed.[9]

Let us return in this light to the problem of our knowledge of the scientific future. Clearly, to identify an insoluble scientific problem we have to show that a certain inherently appropriate scientific question is nevertheless such that its resolution lies beyond every (possible or practicable) state of future science. This is obviously a *very* tall order—particularly so in view of our inevitably deficient grasp of future science. After all, that aspect of the future that is most evidently unknowable is the future of invention, of discovery, of innovation—particularly in the case of science itself. As already noted, Immanuel Kant insisted that every new discovery opens the way to others; every

question that is answered gives rise to yet more questions to be inves-
tigated.[10] Clearly, insofar as this sort of situation obtains, the present
state of science can never answer definitively for that of the future,
since it cannot even predict what questions lie in the agenda.

Another important point must be made regarding this matter of
unpredictability. Great care must be taken to distinguish the ontological and the epistemological dimensions, to keep the entries of
these two columns apart:

Unexplainable	Not (yet) explained
By chance	By some cause we do not know of
Spontaneous	Caused in a way we cannot identify
Random	Lawful in ways we cannot characterize
By whim	For reasons not apparent to us

It is tempting to slide from epistemic incapacity to ontological lawfulness. But we must resist this temptation and distinguish what is
inherently uncognizable from what we just do not happen to cog-
nize. The nature of scientific change makes it inevitably problematic
to slide from present to future incapacity.

After all, science itself sets the limits to predictability, insisting that
some phenomena (the stochastic processes encountered in quantum
physics, for example) are inherently unpredictable. And this is always
to some degree problematic. The most that science can reasonably be
asked to do is to predict what it itself sees as in principle predictable—
to answer every predictive question that it itself countenances as
proper. Thus, if quantum theory is right, the position and velocity of
certain particles cannot be pinpointed conjointly. This renders the following question not insoluble but illegitimate: "What will the exact
position and velocity of particle X be at the exact time t?" Question-
illegitimacy represents a limit that grows out of science itself—a limit
on appropriate questions rather than on available solutions.

And in any case the idea that science might one day be in a position to predict *everything* is simply unworkable. To achieve this, it would be necessary, whenever we predict something, to predict also the effects of making those predictions, and then the ramifications of *those* predictions, and so on ad indefinitum. The very most that can be asked is that science puts us into a position to predict not *everything* but *anything* that we might choose to be interested in and to inquire about.

TEMPORAL FINALITY

Scientists from time to time indulge in eschatological musings and tell us that the scientific venture is approaching its end.[11] And it is, of course, entirely *conceivable* that natural science will come to a stop, and will do so not in consequence of a cessation of intelligent life but in C. S. Peirce's more interesting sense of completion of the project: of eventually reaching a condition after which even indefinitely ongoing inquiry will not—and indeed in the very nature of things *cannot*—produce any significant change, because inquiry has come to the end of the road. The situation would be analogous to that envisaged in the apocryphal story in vogue during the middle 1800s regarding the commissioner of the United States Patents who resigned his post because there was nothing left to invent.[12] Such a position is in theory possible. But here, too, we can never determine that it is actual.

There is no practicable way in which the claim that science has achieved temporal finality can be validated. We can never legitimate an affirmative answer to the question, "Is the current state of science, S, final?" For the prospect of future changes of S can never be precluded. One cannot plausibly move beyond, "We have (in S) no good reason to think that S will ever change," to obtain, "We have (in S) good reason to think that S will never change." To take this posture toward S is to *presuppose its completeness*.[13] It is not simply to take the natural and relatively unproblematic stance that that for which S vouches is to be taken as true but to go beyond this to insist that whatever is true finds a rationalization within S. This argument accordingly embeds *finality* in *completeness*, and in doing so jumps from the frying pan into the fire. For it shifts from what is difficult to what is yet more so. To hold that if something is so at all, then S affords a good reason to take so blatantly ambitious (even megalomaniacal) a view of S that the issue of finality seems almost a harmless appendage.

Moreover, just as the appearance of erotetic and pragmatic equilibrium can be a product of narrowness and weakness, so can temporal finality. We may think that science is unchangeable simply because we have been unable to change it. But that's just not good enough. Were science ever to come to a seeming stop, we could never be sure that it had done so not because it is at the end of the road, but because we are at the end of our tether. We can never ascertain that science has attained the ω-condition of final completion, since from our point of view the possibility of further change lying just around the corner can never be ruled out finally and decisively. No matter how final a position we *appear* to have reached, the prospects of its coming unstuck cannot be precluded. As we have seen, future science is inscrutable. We can never claim with assurance that the position we espouse is immune to change under the impact of further data—that the oscillations are dying out and we are approaching a final limit. In its very nature, science "in the limit" is related to what happens in the long run, and this is something about which we *in principle* cannot gather information: any information we can actually gather inevitably pertains to the short run and not the long run. We can never achieve adequate assurance that *apparent* definitiveness is *real*. We can never consolidate the claim that science has settled into a frozen, changeless pattern. The situation in natural science is such that our knowledge of nature must ever be presumed to be incomplete.

The idea of achieving a state of recognizably completed science is totally unrealistic. Even as widely variant modes of behavior by three dimensional objects could produce exactly the same two-dimensional shadow projections, so very different law systems could in principle engender exactly the same phenomena. We cannot make any definitive inferences from phenomena to the nature of the real. The prospect of perfected science is bound to elude us.

One is thus brought back to the stance of the great Idealist philosophers (Plato, Spinoza, Hegel, Bradley, Royce) that human knowledge inevitably falls short of recognizably perfected science (the Ideas, the Absolute) and must accordingly be looked upon as incomplete. We have no alternative but to proceed on the assumption that the era of innovation is not over—that *future* science can and will prove to be *different* science.

LAW-REVEALING COMPLETENESS

As these deliberations indicate, the conditions of science perfected in point of description, explanation, prediction, and control are all unrealizable. Our information will inevitably prove inconclusive. We have no reasonable alternative to seeing our present-day science as suboptimal, regardless of the question or what date the calendar shows.

Even a system that is finitely complex both in its physical makeup and in its functional laws might nevertheless be infinitely complex in the phenomena that it manifests over time. For the operations of a structurally and lawfully finite system can yet exhibit an infinite intricacy in *productive complexity*, manifesting this limitless diversity in the working out of its processes rather than its spatiostructural composition or the nomic comportment of its basic components. Even if the number of constituents of nature were small, the ways in which they can be combined to yield phenomena in space-time might yet be infinite. Think here of the examples of letters, syllables, words, sentences, paragraphs, books, genres (novels, reference books, etc.), libraries, and library systems. Even a finite nature can, like a typewriter with a limited keyboard, yield an endlessly varied test. It can produce a steady stream of new products—"new" not necessarily in kind but in their functional interrelationships and thus in their theoretical implications. And on this basis our knowledge of nature's workings can be endlessly enhanced and deepened by contemplating an unending proliferation of phenomena.

Moreover, there is no need to assume a ceiling to such a sequence of levels of integrative complexity of phenomenal diversity. The different levels each exhibit an order of their own. The phenomena we attain in the n-th level can have features whose investigation takes us to the $(n + 1)$ level. New phenomena and new laws presumably arise at every level of integrative order. The diverse facets of nature can generate conceptually new strata of operation that yield a potentially unending sequence of levels, each giving rise to its own characteristic principles of organizations, themselves quite unpredictable from the standpoint of the other levels. In this way, even a relatively simple world as regards its basic operations can come to have an effectively infinite cognitive depth, once the notion of a natural phenomenon is broadened to include not just the processes themselves and the products they produce but also the relationship among them.

Consider, for example, some repeatedly exemplified physical feature and contemplate the sequence of 0s and 1s projected according to the rule that the i-th entry in the sequence is 1 if this feature is exemplified on occasion number i, and 0 if not. Whenever two such feature concepts, say C and C', generate such sequences in the manner of

C: 0100110100 . . .

C': 1001011010 . . . ,

then we can introduce the corresponding matching sequence for C and C', 0010010001 . . . , which is such that its i-th position is 1 if the two base sequences agree at their respective i-th positions, and 0 if they disagree. Such matching sequences will have a life of their own. For example, even if two base sequences are random, their matching sequences need not be—for example, when those base sequences simply exchange 0s and 1s. (Even random phenomena can be related by laws of coordination.)

Note that the present discussion does not propound the *ontological* theses that natural science cannot be pragmatically complete or even ω-definitive, but the *epistemological* thesis that science cannot ever be *known to be so*. The point is not that the requirements of definitive knowledge cannot in the nature of things be satisfied but that they cannot be *implemented* (that is, be *shown* to be satisfied). The upshot is that science must always be presumed to be incomplete, not that it necessarily always is so. No doubt this is also true. It cannot, however, be demonstrated on the basis of epistemological general principles.

AN END TO SCIENCE?

Ideal science is not something we have in hand here and now. Nor is it something toward which we are moving along the asymptotic and approximate lines envisaged by C. S. Peirce.[14] Existing science does not and never will embody perfection. The cognitive ideals of completeness, unity, consistency, and definitive finality represent an aspiration rather than a coming reality, an idealized telos rather than a realizable condition of things. Perfected science lies outside history as a useful contrast case that cannot be secured in this imperfect world.

The very unpredictability of future science is a prime indication of inevitable ignorance. After all, scientific inquiry is a venture in inno-vation. Present science can never speak decisively for future science, and present science cannot predict the specific discoveries of future inquiry. Accordingly, claims about what someone will achieve over-all—and thus just where it will be going in the long run—are beyond the reach of attainable knowledge at this or any other particular stage of the scientific state of the art. The idea that there are nondecidable questions that science will never resolve—the Insolubilia Thesis, as we may call it—is something whose truth status can never be settled in a decisive way. And since this is so, this question is self-instantiat-ing: it is a question regarding an aspect of reality (of which science is a part) that scientific inquiry will never—at any specific state of the art—settle decisively.

It should be noted that this issue cannot be settled by supposing a mad scientist who explodes the superbomb that blows the earth to smithereens and extinguishes all organic life as we know it. For the prospect cannot be precluded that intelligent life will evolve else-where. And even if we contemplate the prospect of a "big crunch" that is a reverse "big bang" and implodes our universe into an end, the project can never be precluded that at the other end of the big crunch, so to speak, another era of cosmic development awaits.

In any event, however, while there indeed are scientific insolu-bilia—and we can actually identify some of them—the fact remains that detailed knowledge about the *extent* of our ignorance is unavail-able to us. For what is at stake with this issue of extent is the ratio of the manifold of what one does know to the manifold of that what one does not. And it is impossible in the nature of things to get a fix on the latter. In matters of scientific theorizing, that which is known cannot constrain the lineaments of that which is not.[15]

6

Obstacles to Predictive Foreknowledge

ISSUES OF TEMPORALIZED KNOWLEDGE

The philosophical theologians of the middle ages, who loved puzzles, were wont to exercise their ingenuity regarding this question: "If he is omniscient, does God know what is happening *now*?" And they inclined to answer this question with the response, "yes and no." Clearly an unrestrictedly omniscient God will know everything that happens in the world. And this means that he knows whatever is happening concurrently with the calendar's reading 13 January 2001 and the clock's reading 3:15 P.M. But this is B-series knowledge in McTaggart's terminology—knowledge of events in the manner of before/ concurrent/after. However, as a being who does not occupy a place *within* the manifold of space and time—who, being extra-mundane, lacks the world-internal perspective required for indexicals like here and now—God cannot operate with the correlative concepts, and so in *that* sense, the sense natural to us as mundane world-emplaced creatures who occupy a spatiotemporally qualified position in the world's scheme of things, God does *not* know what is going on *now*. He does not have temporal knowledge in the English philosopher J.M.E. McTaggart's A-series mode of matters in the range of past/present/future. In this regard (as in many others) God is quite unlike ourselves. We finite world-emplaced beings who exist within space-time can ask and answer questions about temporal matters from a time-internal perspective. And this has significant implications for us because *our* knowledge—unlike God's—is something that both has to arise within and be concerned about the temporal domain in the manner of the time-interval perspective of *A*-series temporality. It is, in fact, here that the root source of our cognitive imperfection lies.

This temporal and developmental aspect of knowledge has portentous ramifications. For one thing, it means that we are evidentially incapacitated in comparison with other knowers. Thus consider the yes-or-no question: "When next you yourself (Jones) answer a question, will you do so in the negative?" Whichever way poor Jones replies, he is plunged into error. The best he can do is to plead incapacity and respond, "Can't say." But, of course, third parties are differently circumstanced. *Another* knower—one different from Jones himself—can answer the question by saying, "No, Jones won't do so," and manage to be entirely correct. But this is something that Jones cannot coherently say on his own account. One thing that follows here is that finite knowers are not only not unrestrictedly omniscient, they are not *restrictedly* omniscient either—in the sense of being able to answer correctly every question that another knower can answer.

The temporal aspect of the knowledge of finite beings has other, even more portentous aspects. It means, for one thing, that our knowledge is developmental in nature: that it admits of learning and of discoveries, that there are things (facts) that we do not and cannot know at one temporal juncture that we can and do manage to get to know at another. Knowledge does not come to us from on high, perfected and completed like Athena springing from the head of Zeus. It is the product of a process of inquiry unfolding over time—a process from which the possibilities of error of omission and commission can never be excluded. And this means that problems are bound to arise as our thought contemplates the future.

Our "picture" of the world—our worldview, as one usually calls it—is an epistemic construction built up from our personal and vicarious experience-based knowledge. And like any construction it is made over time from preexisting materials—in this case the information at our disposal. We can select these materials—but only to a limited extent. In the main they force themselves upon us through the channels of our experience. The puzzle question that inevitably arises in this context is that of the accuracy or correctness of our world picture. And it is here that the temporally emplaced aspect of things comes into play.

Perhaps the best way to get a good grip on this issue is by asking how we are to relate the following four items:

1. Presently purported truth: the truth as we ourselves see it, here and now

2. Future truth: the truth as we will come to see it when we push our inquiries further and deeper

3. Completed truth: the truth as we would see it when and if—per impossible—our inquiries were pushed through to the point of ultimate completion

4. Perfected truth: the truth as we ought to come to see it if we conduct our inquiries in a manner definitively appropriate and correct

Presumably we can identify 3 and 4 and regard the result of achieving ideal correctness and completeness as being substantially one and the same. We could thus simply speak here of "the real truth" as realized through the perfecting and completing of inquiry.

However, the real problem is how this authentic truth as per 3 and 4 is to be related to that which we actually have as per 1: our purported truth as it stands here and now.

The few things that can be said here must be said with care and caution. In fact, we do well to proceed *via negativa,* exactly because there is no practicable way of telling *now* exactly what sort of improvements in our presently purported knowledge the *future* progress of inquiry will demand.

THE IMPRACTICABILITY OF AN ALL-PURPOSE PREDICATIVE ENGINE

There can be no question but that the future is a massive reservoir of ignorance. Questions whose resolution requires determining the outcome of contingent future events—future choices and chance occurrences included—are, effectively by definition, not now answerable in a convincingly cogent way. Consider, "How will that coin come out when tossed?" I can, of course, "answer" such a question by simply saying, "Tails." But of course I cannot established the cogency of this answer in a way that will—or should—convince others.

The difficulties that we encounter throughout the predictive realm are deep rooted in the nature of our epistemic situation. And it is instructive to consider the whys and therefores of this circumstance.

Special-purpose instrumentalities for prediction regarding industrial production, earthquakes, the weather, demography, and the like are a familiar part of the present-day scene. But let us imagine the project of combining all such resources together in one great, all-encompassing linkage, implementing the idea of one unrestrictedly versatile and synoptically effective predictive resource. We thus envision creating an all-purpose predictive engine capable—in principle—of resolving any predictive question that one might want to address.

Now suppose that such a project is pursued and issues in the production of the (hypothetical) all-purpose prediction machine *Pythia*. And let us further assume that with the passage of time this machine is ongoingly enhanced and improved. Indeed, let us contemplate the prospect that it is *perfected*. Just what would this mean? How are we to understand perfection in this context of an all-purpose predictor?

The "perfection" at issue here will have two principal aspects: performing without errors of commission (without the *incompetence*-indicative failure of making incorrect predictions) and performing without errors of omission (without the *impotence*-indicative failure of an inability to resolve meaningful predictive questions). We may characterize these two factors as *reliability-perfection* and *versatility-perfection*, respectively.

Now suppose that we have an early model of *Pythia* in hand and that its record of predictive success is respectable but by no means flawless. We ask ourselves: "Will a totally reliable *Pythia* be developed by the year 2500—one that is error free, so that it never makes an incorrect prediction?" We can certainly wonder about this predictive question. And it is clear that a negative answer here could eventually be disconfirmed when that future *Pythia* malfunctions. *But a positive answer can never be validated.* We can, of course, *evidentiate* this claim to perfection to some (modest) extent though a record of predictive success. But we can never actually *verify* it in the sense of definitively establishing its truth. For—obviously—the prospect of failure with an unasked question can never be set aside on the basis of information actually obtainable by us at any given time. The prospect of *Pythia*'s luck—or, rather, competence—running out at some point can never be excluded.

There is, to be sure, the intriguing prospect of putting to *Pythia* the predictive question: "Are you reliability imperfect—that is, will you ever at some point in the future come up with an incorrect prediction?" It is clear that we could gain but little added confidence from a reassuringly negative answer here. Future error would now just transmute into present error as well. And of course we have no way to check up on it. Claims to reliability-perfection are always indecisive. They can never be satisfactorily substantiated irrespective of whether they are made by us (the manufacturers and users of *Pythia*) or by *Pythia* itself.

Now on to versatility perfection. Could *Pythia* possibly predict *everything*? Could it provide a tenable answer for *every* predictive question one cares enough to ask? Clearly not. For one thing, there are essentially paradoxical questions on the lines of, "What is a predictive question that you will never ever have to deal with in answering questions put to you?" *Pythia* must keep silent on this issue or else confess its completeness imperfection with an honest "Can't say." But the question itself is certainly not meaningless, since we ourselves or some other predictor could in principle answer it correctly.

Again, we could wire our supposedly perfect predictor up to a bomb in such a way that it would be blown to smithereens when next it answers "Yes." And we now ask it, "Will you continue active and functioning after giving your next answer?" Should it answer "Yes," it would be blasted to bits and its answer thereby falsified. Should it answer "No," it would (*ex hypothesi*) continue in operation and its answer thereby falsified. Viability can be achieved here only by letting the predictor have the option of responding "Can't say" at its disposal—and accordingly fail to be completeness-perfected. For some predictive questions are unresolvable as a matter of practical reality. ("Where will the last man ever to think about Napoleon be born?") Others are so as a matter of general theory. (For example, "How long will you need to resolve this number-theoretic question?"—the question asked of a computer concerning the arithmetical questions at issue with Alan Turing's intractable "halting problem.") No predictor is immune from failure.

To say that a predictive question is unresolvable is not, of course, to say that a predictor cannot answer it. We could certainly program a predictive machine to answer every yes/no question by "Yes," every *name* question by "George Washington," every *when* question by "In ten minutes," and so on. If it is simply an answer that we want, we can contrive predictors that will oblige us. But the problem, of course, is to have a predictor whose predictions are *probable* or, in the case of a putatively perfect predictor, *correct*—on a basis that is credible in advance of the fact.

Specifically, one of the issues regarding which no predictor can ever function perfectly is its own predictive performance. For example, consider asking that putatively perfect predictor the following question:

> Will you answer this question—this *very* question—by an apologetic "Can't say" rather than "Yes" or "No"?

We arrive here at the following situation:

The answer given is	Its truth-status is automatically	So the predictor
Yes	False	Fails (by falsity)
No	False	Fails (by falsity)
Can't say	Immaterial	Fails (by indecision)

Our supposedly perfect predictor will inevitably fail to function adequately.

The long and short of it is that no predictor can function adequately with respect to its own operations and, in particular, none can predict its own future predictions. The very most one could plausibly ask for might seem to be that *predictors predict correctly everything that is in principle possible for them to predict*. But even here there are problems. Perhaps the most obvious of them is that of deciding just what is in principle possible for a predictor by way of genuine prediction. For to determine what is in theory or in principle predictable—and what is not—we have to look to the deliverances of natural science. For science itself tells us that some sorts of predictions are in principle infeasible—for example, the outcome of such quantum processes as are at issue in the question, "Exactly when will this atom of a transuranic element with the half-life of 283 years disintegrate?" "Exactly what will be the position and momentum of this particle two minutes from now?" What is needed at this point is a determination of *what is in fact predictable*—and not just an indication of what the science of the day *considers (perhaps mistakenly) to be predictable*. And this is an issue that could only be settled satisfactorily by perfected or completed science, something we do not have now and could not be sure of having even if *(per impossible)* we did sometime acquire it. We have to come to terms with the frustrating but unavoidable circularity inherent in the holistic aspect of cognitive justification: predictive perfection would require scientific or explanatory perfection, and such perfection could only be validated via predictive perfection.

Moreover, it is readily demonstrated that every predictor (natural or artificial) has blindspots: it must sometimes answer "Can't say," even where *another* predictor can quite appropriately respond "Yes" or "No." This circumstance emerges from the following predictive question:

> Q: Will the register of predictive questions that you,
> *Pythia*, will resolve affirmatively this year ultimately
> *omit* (that is, fail to include) this very question Q itself?

Clearly, this question will drive *Pythia* into perplexity. Suppose for the sake of deliberation that the question is answered "Yes." Then Q is a predictive question that *Pythia* answers affirmatively and which must therefore itself feature on the register at issue—which is exactly what that affirmative answer denies. So in this case, *Pythia* has answered our predictive question incorrectly. On the other hand, suppose that the question is answered "No." Then, given the substance of Q, the register of affirmatively resolved predictive questions will have to omit Q, so that, in consequence, the proper answer is "Yes." Here, too, *Pythia* has answered our predictive question incorrectly. (The situation is summarized in table 6.1; note that the first and last columns systematically conflict here.) With no prospect of a correct answer in the yes/no range, *Pythia*'s best—indeed only—error-avoiding option is to make the incapacity-acknowledging response "Can't say." (In this way, every predictor is unavoidably versatility-imperfect.) But observe that this is *not* an issue on which rational prediction is inherently impossible. We ourselves could perfectly well give an affirmative answer—and could well be correct in doing so. It is essential to the paradoxical aspect of our hypothetical situation that this question of predictive performance is addressed to the predictor itself; reflexivity is a crucial factor here.

The long and short of it is that every predictor is bound to manifest versatility-incapacities with respect to it own predictive operations. A "perfected predictor" that correctly answers every meaningful and answerable predictive question—those regarding its own operations included—is a logico-conceptual impossibility.

After all, what would a perfect predictor have to be like? What would it have to be able to do to deserve this designation? There are several alternatives. We could require it to be able to do the following correctly:

1. Predict everything.

2. Predict everything that is possible (for *some* predictor or other) to predict (in the prevailing circumstances).

3. Predict everything that it is theoretically possible for it itself (in its actual circumstances) to predict.

We have seen that requirement 1 is inappropriate, since there are certain eventuations that, even in theory, a predictor could not possibly predict in a rationally cogent way (e.g., the outcomes of stochastic processes). Moreover, we have seen that even requirement 2 is inappropriate, since there are certain eventuations that, even in theory, a predictor could not rationally predict regarding its own operations but which *another* predictor might well be able to foretell. Thus all one could plausibly ask for is perfection in the sense of requirement 3. And yet even here there are problems. For even if we had at our disposal a perfected predictor in *this* limited sense, we would never be able to determine satisfactorily that it was so.

The idea of a perfected all-purpose predictive engine accordingly comes to grief. To be able to make credible predictions about the operations of one predictive engine we will need another. But even two will not do. A cyclic setup with *A* answering predictive questions about *B*'s performance and *B* about *A*'s will also eventuate in paradox. We would, in fact, have to launch into an infinite regress here.

The very most that one could sensibly ask of a predictive device— singly or in the aggregate—is to perform in a way that is and has been error free *as far as one can presently tell* and that this performance is "miraculously" effective in point of versatility. We could, without actual absurdity, ask that a predictor manifest an *amazingly competent* performance. But it lies in the nature of things that we cannot reasonably demand *perfection*.

THE EPISTEMOLOGICAL AND ONTOLOGICAL LIMITS OF PREDICTABILITY

One can evaluate predictors comparatively by looking at how they perform in relation to others. But one can also try to access them absolutely by comparing actual performance with what is in theory possible. But this, of course, requires determining where the limits of the possible lie, and here the issue of obstacles comes to the fore.

In principle there are both ontological and epistemological limits to predictive foreknowledge, and obstacles to successful prediction can reside either in the nature of things or in our own cognitive limitations. Ontological limits exist insofar as the future of the domain at issue is *developmentally open*—causally undetermined or underdetermined by the existing realities of the present and open to the development of wholly unprecedented patterns owing to the contingencies of choice, chance, and chaos. Epistemological limits on prediction exist insofar as the future is *cognitively inaccessible*—either because we cannot secure the needed data, or because it is impossible for us to discover the operative laws, or even possibly because the requisite inferences and/or calculations involve complexities that outrun the reach of our capabilities.

As this view of the matter suggests, the project of rational prediction can be frustrated in various ways. Specifically, the principal impediments to predictability are the following:

1. Anarchy: literal lawlessness—the absence of lawful regularities to serve as linking mechanisms

2. Volatility: the absence of nomic stability and thus of cognitively manageable laws

3. Uncertainty: law-ignorance—the lack of nomic information due to an epistemic failure on our part in securing information about the operative linking mechanisms

4. Haphazard: the lawful linking mechanisms (such as they are) do not permit the secure inference of particular conclusions but leave outcomes undermined owing to the operation of:

   Chance and chaos: stochastic or random processes that make the laws at issue irretrievably probabilistic

> Arbitrary choice: determinations that are essentially groundless and are thus rationally intractable
>
> Innovation: the entry of novelty in ways that make outcomes unforeseeable because prediscernible patterns are continually broken

5. Fuzziness: data indetermination—the inherent (ontological) indefiniteness of the quantities at issues in the data—whether individually or in a collectively conjugate way)

6. Myopia: data ignorance—the lack of an adequate detailing of the data inherent in an epistemic incapacity to secure the requisite information in sufficient volume and detail

7. Inferential incapacity: the infeasibility of carrying out the needed reasoning (inferences/calculations)—even where we may have the requisite data and know the operative inferential linkages

These various prediction-impending factors require closer inspection. Let us begin with anarchy and instability.

The situation where there just are no laws—rather than there being mere ignorance about them—is clearly fatal for prediction. Here impredictability roots in the condition of genuine anarchy obtaining where we face a state of actual patternlessness—unruliness in which (within the range of possibilities at issue) *anything* might happen. It is clear that in such situations no determinate outcome can be arrived at through warranted inference: the future conditions and states of such a domain just cannot be foreseen on the basis of data relating to its past. Not that plausible prediction is altogether impossible with anarchic systems: we can safely predict that they will keep on being anarchic, since no order-engendering processes are (by hypothesis) at work.

Next to outright anarchy there stands volatility and instability of patterns, which also function as a major obstacle to prediction. As we have seen, rational predictability requires stable transtemporal coordination relationships—discernible patterns of lawful regularity that link the past and present condition of the phenomena at issue, where alone the *observational* determination is possible, with their future state. Prediction is—clearly—easiest where innovation is snail paced. The river system of the country will not be all that different in generations hence. But its road system is something else again—not to speak of its communication system. Again, the prediction of economic and business conditions in the United States was far easier in the 1960s than in the 1970s and 1980s because of the greater stability of economic conditions during the former decade. In general, it is clear that in a world whose modus operandi is radically variable and innovative, the established patterns of the past that survive into the long-term future will fade away to a point where long-term prediction is virtually impossible.

An important difference is neatly marked in English usage by the difference between *unpredictable* and *impredictable*, the former being geared to volatility, the latter to intractability. In London weather conditions are unpredictable in March: one minute it can be clear and sunny and ten minutes later there may be clouds and rain. Here instability is at work. On the other hand, the future of American poetry is impredictable: we simply have no grip on any laws or regularities that provide for rational prediction. But both cases alike frustrate the project of prediction.

To be sure, predictability does not require the lawful stability of *phenomena* but rather the lawful stability of *process*. Consider the series 1, 2, 2, 3, 3, 3, 4, 4, 4, 4, etc. There are no periodicities, no ever-recurrent groups or constellations of phenomena. But of course there is a very simple *regularity pattern* among the phenomena, one that is encapsulated in the rule: *Repeat the i-th integer i times in succession.* It is the existence of *rule-governed patterns*—rather than any need for actual cycles and explicit periodicities—that lies at the heart of the lawful regularity essential to prediction. The predictability of the future is subject to the requirement that the world's modus operandi can be characterized (at least in substantial part) by such nomic principles—and thus on the extent to which the world's processes are lawful in exhibiting patterns that manifest a conformity to rules. Irregularity of phenomena is compatible with prediction-admitting lawfulness, but irregularity of process—the eccentricity of modus operandi at issue in anarchy—precludes rational prediction. A world without a stable order—even if only a probabilistic one—must inevitably fail to be predictively tractable.

Where does our world stand on this regard? Modern physics depicts nature as a terrain that contains widespread pockets of stability within a larger environment of cognitively unmanageable instability—a realm in which the possibilities of prediction are decidedly limited in scope. The prospects of prediction are clearly compromised in situations where the phenomenology at issue is sufficiently irregular that discernible patterns change erratically, so that stable laws are unavailable because the rules of the game keep changing in ways not stably related to what has gone by in the past. And just here lies the problem with this real world of ours. Prediction over the extremely short term is easy—things remain just the same. Prediction over the extremely long term is effectively impossible. Who can say what will succeed the cosmic collapse that some versions of big bang cosmology hold in store? We inhabit the predictively difficult realm in between—the halfway house between nanoseconds and cosmic eons in which our human lot is cast. At every level of scale in cosmic organization—the atomic, the biological, the cosmic—we seem to encounter a mixture of stability and instability, of order and anarchy, of regularly and fluctuation of predictability and unpredictability.

> It seems to me that it cannot happen even with God him-
> self that he should know what is going to happen acciden-
> tally and by chance (*casu et fortuito*). For if he knows, then
> it is certain that this will be, and if this is certain then
> chance does not exist. But chance does exist, and so there
> is no foreknowledge of things that happen by chance. (*De
> Divinatione*, II, vii, 18)

This argumentation effectively shows that genuine chance (if and
where it exists) precludes for-certain predictability. Where chance is
at work, the world can exhibit a fixed past and nevertheless confront
us with distinct but altogether feasible futures—situations that are
descriptively indistinguishable may unfold in different ways and issue totally different results. If we were to "replay" history in such
situations—be it natural or human history—we could, and most
likely would, arrive at ultimate results that represent different (and
potentially *radically* different) developments.

Chance makes for an unruliness in the phenomena themselves,
because the processes at issue are *stochastic* (chance-involving) in not
conforming to any sort of definite, outcome-determinative rule. Not
that we cannot—by lucky guesswork—successfully predict eventuations that are due to chance. It is just that we cannot do so more successfully than the probabilistic nature of the case admits of. When
you toss a fair coin, chance alone determines heads or tails. And
while you may be lucky and happen to make the correct guess, it lies
on the nature of the case that over the long run you cannot manage
it more than half of the time.

To be sure, some developments may be characterized as matters of chance in a related but decidedly weaker sense—it is not that
they fail to fit within the outcome-determinative cause-and-effect
matrix of events, but rather that they depart from the way in which
affairs *usually* proceed in the domain of phenomena at issue. They

lie outside the *normal* course of things in the domain at issue, so that the usual bets are off. (A good example in human affairs would be the assassination of a key political figure.) Strict chance means that the actual laws of nature fail to be decisively future-determinative; "chance" in this weaker sense means only that the *usual and familiar* regularities fail to be so.

A *deterministic* world is one where chance plays no part at all—one that is (*in principle*) completely predictable so that *every* predictive question can in theory be answered, leaving no room for surprises. The world is like a film where every frame is programmed in advance. With such a world one can dispense with probabilistic considerations because predictive issues can in theory always be settled decisively one way or another. But to whatever extent a world falls short of this idealized state—as this world of ours to all appearances does—its indeterminism opens the door to impredictability.

Many theorists have seen chance as a paramount factor in the world. Indeed, the Greek atomists attributed *everything* that happens in the world to pure chance. In this they were opposed by the Stoics, who taught that *nothing* happens by chance because the order of nature's lawfulness is all-determinative. By contrast the Epicureans espoused a mixed theory of chance-law combination that portrayed the world as a halfway house in this regard. And modern physics takes this intermediate, Epicurean line here. Acknowledging the role of chance and stochastic randomness in the world's eventuations, it focuses on those physical phenomena that are inherently probabilistic. From the perspective of modern physics, the centrality of stochastic processes spread in nature has thrown a barrier across the prospect of unfettered predictability and forced us to turn from exact forecasts to probability distributions. In particular, quantum phenomena, being of a fundamentally stochastic nature, vividly manifest the ontological side of impredictability. Here science itself insists that there are predictions we should not ask for. Thus, assuming that present-day physics has it right, we must not (for example) ask for a prediction of the time when a certain atom of a transuranic element will disintegrate, because such a time can in principle not be predetermined. And, of course, the operation of chance in science is not confined to physics alone. In biology we see random processes at work in genetics (mutations), in economics there is the random walk theory of stock market price fluctuation, and so on. Chance is ubiquitously present upon the stage of modern science: witness the diffusion of probabilistic and statistical techniques throughout this domain. And chance, as Cicero already taught, brings impredictability in its wake.

On the telling of modern science, then, the laws of nature delimit and circumscribe the course of events but do not all-pervasively decide it. Natural history is like chess: In chess the players decide within the framework of rules, and this means that a great deal can be predicted. But not, of course, everything. The contingency introduced through the decision of the players also comes into it. Analogously, the world's realities leave room for the irreducible contingency of chance determinations. In the long run we are all dead (as Keynes observed), but the exact details—the timing and manner of our demise—are (to all appearances) not appointed in advance by the fabric of natural law and are, to this extent, impredictable.

To be sure, chance and predictability are not all-out antagonists. For probabilistically geared prediction that forgoes claims to certainty is something else again. In a gas where millions of atoms are knocking about randomly, we cannot say what any one of them would do, but we can manage to do statistical mechanics in the aggregate. Individual chance events are indeed unpredictable, but the very randomness of chance fluctuation means that large-scale phenomenology will be predictable via the laws of chance codified in probability theory. A chance or random sequence of (say) digits is thereby bound to have a very definite statistical structure: there is no chance without a statistical order of a very definite sort. Thus, while chance *can* obviously block the path for prediction, it certainly need not necessarily do so. In quantum theory—for example—it is eminently unlikely that an atom with a half-life of a week would still be there—unchanged after as before—a year later on. We therefore could—and would—confidently predict that it would not be. What is lacking here is not predictability itself, but only the fail-proof certainty of for-sure prediction.

MORE ON CHANCE, UNCERTAINTY, AND CHAOS

However, while the net effect of chance and uncertainty is the same either way as far as predictability goes—namely, incapacitation—these two factors clearly represent very different conditions. With chance, the impredictability roots in something we do (or could) actually know, namely that the phenomena at issue are genuinely stochastic (chance-driven). With uncertainty, by contrast, the incapacity to predict is grounded in a *lack* of information—in our inability to say how the relevant phenomenology operates.

The two prediction-spoilers are very different: the one ontological, the other epistemological. However, despite this theoretical difference, there is often a *cognitive* (rather than *optical*) *illusion* at work to make ignorance look like chance. The Fallacy of Misattributed Chance looms large. When the laws governing the phenomena are too complex for ready apprehension, then it is all too easy to ascribe eventuations to chance and thereby attribute to nature the effects of our own cognitive deficiencies.

A physical system is said to be *chaotic* when its processes are so extremely volatile that very minute differences in an initial state—differences so small as to lie beneath the threshold of discrimination—can nevertheless engender very great differences in result, with minuscule local variations amplifying into substantially different eventual outcomes. The flow pattern of cigarette smoke in a room, or the motion of an inflated toy balloon released with open end, are typical examples. Here even the most exacting *feasible* measurement of initial conditions would not be sufficiently precise to make it possible to determine the exact patterns of motion. In such cases, even a system whose laws are altogether deterministic—that is, whose *future* state-parameter values are in theory computable on the basis of its present state-parameter values—excludes the prospect of prediction since it is effectively infeasible to effect with the requisite accuracy the measurements of those needed initial state-parameter values. The weather affords a good example. As one exposition puts it:

> Why have the meteorologists such difficulty in predicting the weather? Why do the rains, the storms themselves seem to us to come by chance, so that many persons find it quite ridiculous to pray for an eclipse? We see that great perturbations generally happen in regions where the atmosphere is in unstable equilibrium. The meteorologists are aware that this equilibrium is unstable, that a cyclone is arising somewhere; but where they cannot tell; one-tenth of a degree more or less at any point, and the cyclone bursts here and not there, and spreads its ravages over countries which it would have spared. This we could have foreseen if we had known that tenth of a degree, but the observations were neither sufficiently close nor sufficiently precise, and for this reason all seems due to the agency of chance.

Of course, context proves crucial here. In a setting where the weather falls into relatively stable and discernible patterns—southern California, for example—meteorological prediction is easy. But in the more turbulent conditions of more northerly latitudes the situation is very different.

Chaos often masquerades as chance, seeing that no practicable efforts on our part can yield satisfactory predictive results. For with chaos there is an ineliminable prospect that circumstances that we do not—and cannot—ascertain may nevertheless make all the difference in the world for the phenomena at issue. But there is an important theoretical difference here. A process is indeterministic if *literally identical* initial conditions (i.e., one selfsame circumstantial state of affairs) can eventuate in different results. By contrast, a process is chaotic if *observationally indistinguishable* initial conditions can eventuate in different results, irrespective of how sophisticatedly we make our observations—within the limits of practicability—that is, short of unrealizable idealizations. Here, very small differences in input—differences so small as to be beneath the threshold of detectability by any available means—can become amplified into substantial differences in outcome. And even a minute variation in one's determination of a system's initial state can make for a complete blur in one's predictive vision of future conditions. This means that no physical or conceptual model that we could ever make of a chaotic process (whose condition would, after all, always at some point differ from those of the system in some minuscule way) could ever be used as an instrument for reliable prediction. Such chaos is by no means an uncommon situation in nature—witness the descent of lightning, the fall of leaves, swirl of tobacco smoke, or the diffusion of plague. In many causal processes, factors that are prima facie so minute as to be undetectable can become amplified to the point of making an enormous difference in the course of events. A small twinge can cause a person to misstep and slip into the way of an onrushing omnibus. A tiny muscle spasm can lead us to cough out a germ that would otherwise have killed us. The slightest change in timing can make the difference between buying a winning or losing lottery ticket. Such chaotic factors are yet another source of impredictability. Along with chance and ignorance, chaos means that luck—that is, the impetus of unforeseeability on matters of human weal and woe—comes to play a major role in our affairs.

Epistemic theorists have been inclined to neglect this issue of chance versus chaos. Focusing too intently on the extent to which the future is knowable in principle or in theory through the operation of deterministic (nonprobabilistic) laws, they forget about the issue of data accessibility and thus address a foreknowledge that is divine (idealized) rather than human (physically practicable) in its power. They fail to realize that prediction can be infeasible even in a world ruled in detail by a system of deterministic laws whose nature we actually know.

SPONTANEITY, CHOICE, AND FREE WILL

Systems whose development is self-determined and whose activities proceed in ways engendered autonomously from within the system in ways at least partly independent of the external circumstances—systems whose operation is, at least in part, *spontaneous*—will for this very reason function in ways that are not completely predictable for external observers. For where the course of developments is shaped by externally unmonitorable inner processes, prediction becomes infeasible. Human choice is a particularly striking example of this phenomenon. Let us consider briefly some of its predictive ramifications.

To be genuinely human is to be, in at least some degree, a free and independent agent—to be other than an automaton and accordingly to have the prospect of making choices without any external determination or constraint. For what their free will generally has people do is not to choose arbitrarily unpredictably in the ordinary range of cases but to do so in at least some extraordinary ones. Jean Buridan's classic example may well be right—an ass may conceivably starve between two equally appealing bales of hay. But a human free agent will certainly not do so. Or again, in suitable circumstances we may "choose" to put our free will into suspension and hand over the selection among alternatives to an impredictable random device—say a coin toss. It is less the operation of our free will than the prospect of our deliberate suspension of its operations that can render human actions unpredictable. (I can freely delegate my choice in various interactions to the outcome of a coin toss.) Free will can thus be deployed so as to defeat prediction. Once I realize that a predictor forecasts that I shall act in a certain way, I can deliberately defeat this by refraining from doing so—though this may well mean that I shall have to cut off my own nose to spite this predictive pest.

To be sure, having free will does *not* render one's actions automatically unpredictable. After all, there is no phenomenological (observational) difference between a regularity engendered by a preprogrammed mechanism and one that is produced by a free agent who has (freely) decided upon following some rule or forming some habit. Moreover, intelligent agents are in a privileged position where the prediction of their own actions is concerned. Then, too, we can perfectly well predict—though often only in somewhat general terms—how the people we know well will react when threatened, endangered, offended, or flattered. If I know your taste in books or in moving pictures, then I can confidently predict your selections among alternatives—and will probably be right much of the time. And in general we can safely predict of a sensible person that she will freely choose to do those things which are, under the circumstances, the sensible things to do. Accordingly, the operation of a power of free choice certainly does not mean that there *must* be impredictability—only that there *can* be.

As is generally the case, God will be an exception here, seeing that he is supposed to be able to predict everything. But St. Augustine was entirely right to maintain that God's foreknowledge does not abrogate man's possession of free will, seeing that what God must be supposed to foreknow is simply how we in fact go about putting that free will to work. Even if God has realized from the beginning of time what we would do in resolving our choices, this has no effect on us—and could not do so since he could not tell us without altering that postulated choice situation beyond recognition.

For presently relevant concerns—and indeed for all *practical* purposes—a "compatibilist" view of the relationship between predictability and human freedom accordingly makes perfectly good sense. On such an approach, an individual's act is to be seen as free not through its being exempt from the prediction-admitting order of causality, but through its being *internally produced* through the agent's own decisions, resolutions, and choices. Free agency consists in voluntary action, in the capacity to act as one chooses. And the circumstance that one's wishes and preferences may themselves somehow be determined would nowise abrogate that freedom as long as that causal determination is in substantial measure *internal*. Such a determination by reasons is emphatically not at odds with freedom, but rather constitutes a manifestation of it. Accordingly, even genuinely free acts may well be—and generally are—confidently predictable on the basis of the orderly modus operandi of an agent's internal causation in the order of thought. Since the actions of rational agents are governed by their goals, desires, inclinations, etc., one can—in principle—develop sufficient data to make confident predictability a perfectly real prospect here.

The idea of rationality and its ramifications thus provides us with a very important and useful predictive instrument in the context of human activities. Determining what it is that, from the angle of *their* aims and values, is the most advantageous thing for people to do provides an eminently effective device for predicting their comportment. But of course the presumption of rational competence is crucial here. After all, with calculations there is in general only one way of getting it right but zillions of ways of getting it wrong. We thus find it comparatively easy to predict what a competent mathematician would arrive at but would find it very hard indeed to say just what a highly *incompetent* mathematician would come up with.

To be sure, even where agents behave in erratic and impredictable ways, this need not preclude predictive foreknowledge in the large. For as long as those eccentricities cancel out in the statistical aggregate or become lost in a statistical fog, we can obtain perfectly stable large-scale aggregate effects. The growth of a snowflake is chaotic but must always yield six points. Automobile accidents occur with randomness but yield relatively stable occurrence rates. And, as macroeconomics indicates, the impredictability of free agents in some aspect of their individual comportment is perfectly compatible with the predictability of large-scale, aggregate effects. The salient consideration as regards predictability is not that free agents are thereby unpredictable, but rather that they *can* be so. For as the example of Buridan's ass shows, an agent can effect decisions even in all absence of reason—and do so without providing clues for others to make use of. Having the option of being comparatively opaque to predictive insight by others is one of the salient characteristics of free agency. And being in a better position than others to establish a good predictive record regarding one's self-comportment is yet another.

INNOVATION

Innovation—invention or discovery—often carries impredictability in its wake, seeing that predictability feeds on stability and innovation by definition breaks with the established order of things. Both nature and intelligent agents *invent* new things—and these novelties can be genuinely creative through engendering objects, processes, or states that are totally unlike anything that has gone before. The temporal course of things creates new realities—new *physical* realities with the evolution of astronomical or biological objects and new *ideational* realities with the birth of new concepts and ideas. And it lies deep in the nature of genuine innovation that it precludes foreseeability through abrogating the preexisting order of things and changing the rules of the game. There is no earthly way we can foresee the political structures or slang expressions that will be used in the year 3000.

Innovation can take very different forms. The types of innovation that principally concern us are the following:

- Ontological: new things, processes, products, states of affairs. (Note: "new" in the presently operative sense will mean new *in kind*)

- Phenomenal: new types of events or courses of events—new natural or personal histories

- Epistemic (or conceptual or cognitive): new sorts of knowledge, ideas, information, problems, questions

Epistemic novelty is perhaps the predictively least accessible mode of innovation. In particular, the course of discovery—of cognitive innovation—is a major source of predictive incapacity. For the fruits of human ingenuity always come as a surprise (and frequently an unwelcome one). If rational foresight could anticipate its operations, creativity as such would not exist. The historian can say that "X was the first person to state (or realize) that the human body consists principally of water," but no predictive sage could have foretold in advance that "X will be the first person to state (or realize) that the human body consists principally of water." Such prediction will be automatically self-falsifying because the claim at issue is literally paradoxical. Human creativity and inventiveness defies predictive foresight. We know full well *that* there will be unforeseen innovations in art, literature, technology, science, business, and other large-scale areas of human endeavor in the decades and centuries ahead. But of course we cannot predict *what* they will be.

FUZZINESS: PROBLEMS OF QUANTUM INDETERMINISM

The discovery of nature's fuzzy character at the level of submicroscopic detail in quantum physics has been one of the great intellectual triumphs of twentieth-century physics. The physical world, as quantum theory sees it, is characterized by two sorts of "incompleteness":

1. Outcome underdetermination: "collapse of the wave packet." The theory specifies a distribution of probabilities across possible observable outcomes of quantum transactions but excludes the prospect of predetermining the definite particular outcome that is ultimately observed to occur. The outcomes are inherently stochastic (i.e., chance-driven), and physically indistinguishable states can issue in different results. Individually they cannot be predicted with certainty, all we can do is treat the issue statistically and predict the distribution of outcomes over numerous individual cases.

2. Descriptive nonspecificity: "conjugate parameters." The theory holds that certain interrelated characteristics of quantum-scale particles (specifically position and momentum) are such that as we measure one more accurately, our capacity to measure the other will deteriorate: the one parameter-determination becomes unmanageable to the extent that one succeeds in fixing the other. Imprecision can be deflected from one to the other, but not eliminated from the pair. The two variables are so interrelated that the imprecision-variation of the one

(Δx) can only be decreased beyond a certain point at the cost of increasing that of the other (Δy). That is, their multiplicative product cannot be diminished below a certain fixed level, so that we always have:

$\Delta x \, \Delta y > q$, for some fixed quantity q.

As of a certain point, these qualities stand in a "teeter-totter" relationship, where raising the one involves lowering the other. Accordingly, quantum theory has it that we should not ask for a prediction of both the exact position and the exact momentum of a certain electron at some future time, because such conjugate parameters are so interconnected that they cannot *in principle* be conjointly specified with precision.

Insofar as this sector of physical theory is correct, two sorts of predictive infeasibility are thus destined to obtain at the quantum level: (1) one cannot predict certain individual outcomes with certainty, (2) one cannot predict certain parameter values conjointly. In consequence, chance enters into nature's operation in a way that means that some predictive questions will always prove unanswerable. Nature's distillation of an actual observation out of the fuzziness of quantum reality always has processes for which the theory itself makes no provision. Moreover, the theory insists that both of these features are inherent aspects of the physical realm: as most quantum theorists see it, they represent objective characteristics of physical reality and not mere cognitive incapacities on our part to effect certain determinations.

The first of these quantum "incompletenesses"—observation underdetermination—means that the determinism of classical physics shatters against the irreducibly probabilistic nature of quantum phenomena, a circumstance that spells the inherent incompleteness of physics because it precludes the physical condition of the present from constraining a particular outcome for the future. And the second sort of "incompleteness"—descriptive nonspecificity—means that in some circumstances our ability to answer one predictive question conflicts with our ability to answer another, with some predictive issues manageable only at the cost of subverting the manageability of others. This state of affairs puts us into the anomalous-seeming position of making us choose which quantities we would like to predict with detailed accuracy, seeing that the choice of one possibility here automatically precludes that of another. The predictive telescope by whose means we peer into the future has a variable focus, as it were, and bringing sharpness to some details impels others into fuzzy obscurity.

Fortunately, the impredictability that inheres in the fuzziness of the quantum domain is a special and rather limited sort that generally washes out with statistical aggregation. It characterizes one particular level of reality and is not something that we encounter with comparable frequency in large-scale sections of nature—and certainly not in everyday life. All the same, the stochastic/probabilistic aspect of quantum phenomena does illustrate both the need for probabilistic mechanisms in the theory of prediction and the categorical infeasibility of a scientifically warranted prediction of certain features of the real world.

MYOPIA

A related problem arises when the predictively requisite data cannot be acquired on a sufficiently timely basis. After all, the data acquisition of any sort—be it observation or measurement or whatever—requires the deployment of real effort and resources in real time, and if this process cannot in practice be accomplished in a sufficiently timely way, then prediction becomes impracticable.

In particular, substantial problems arise in many predictive situations where there is a mismatch between the parameters that figure in the theories needed for prediction and the parameters that can actually be observed and measured. (In economics, for example, we cannot *directly* measure the circulation velocity of money or the overall employment rate of the workforce—these are values which will have to be estimated, via sampling and other procedures, on the basis of other, more practicable measurements.) In such situations we cannot use *actual* but only *estimated* parameter values for our predictive purposes. And many different sorts of errors can enter in with this estimation process: errors in sampling technique, in measurement, in factual interpretation, etc. And such errors in our estimates will often engender greatly amplified errors in the predictive inferences we draw from them, particularly so when many different quantities are involved. To predict how well the whole team will play, I may well need to develop individual predictions about each of its players, and the result can be a matter of piling error upon error.

Fortunately, the fluctuations that arise here may "work out" over large aggregates so that statistical prediction over the larger scale may still be possible even where we cannot secure individualized detail. The insurance company does not have a clue about how long Jones (age forty) or Robinson (age fifty) will live. But it does know pretty firmly that within the whole group of its clients a certain percentage of the forty-year-olds and a somewhat larger percentage of the fifty-year-olds will die within the next five years. After all, prediction becomes easier with aggregate phenomena, since in statistical aggregation we often cancel out the vagaries of individual fluctuations to produce a stable overall result. When this occurs, prediction becomes a prospect once more, myopia in matters of detail notwithstanding.

Sometimes, moreover, a predictive outcome can be insensitive to errors in the data. Suppose the question is whether a certain apparently healthy person whom we met the other day will be alive one hundred years hence. You think she is about thirty years old, while I estimate her age at fifty. Still, the negative answer to our predictive question will be pretty much unaffected either way—and much the same holds if the question is whether she will be alive five days hence. Here the details of the data surely do not matter. Unfortunately, however, the predictive questions that interest us all too frequently relate to issues that are highly data sensitive, so that myopia becomes a serious matter that carries ignorance in its wake.

FACTOR EXFOLIATION AND IMPREDICTABILITY DIFFUSION

Predictive issues are often multifaceted, involving a plurality of issues (what, when, where, how) in circumstances where effective prediction involves getting *all* of these facets right. And this may prove to be difficult or impossible. The predictive situation that confronted the U.S. military intelligence establishment in the run-up to the Japanese attack on Pearl Harbor in December 1941 is instructive in this regard. The question, "Were the Japanese about to go to war?" posed no problem for U.S. intelligence: all concerned were perfectly clear that the answer was "Yes." "*When* were they going to strike?" posed no problems either: all concerned knew that it was just a matter of days after 27 November. The only real problem was related to the question, "*Where* are they going to strike?" Here the performance was more mixed. The intelligence establishment agreed that attacks would be launched in the direction of the British, Dutch, and French territories in the South Pacific—no error of commission there. The only error was one of omission. Nobody had an inkling that Pearl Harbor would be attacked, a step that was seen not only as overly risky for the Japanese because of the chances of an attack fleet being sighted en route, but also as infeasible for technical reasons, since the harbor was thought too shallow for the air-launched torpedoes needed to cripple the warships at anchor.

When effective prediction requires the resolution of various sub-ordinated issues, we may have a situation where the chain is no stronger than its weakest link. For if any one of a multitude of operative factors is predictively intractable, the whole problem remains unresolved. Where the overall issue is systemically holistic, malfunction in a single component may well engender an overall breakdown.

Predictability thus runs into difficulty whenever the causality of the issue sensitively involves several difficult-to-determine factors that themselves depend on others of a like nature. Take, for example, the question, "Will the world's food supply be adequate in the year 3000?" Resolving this predictive issue in a sensible way requires the predictive assessment of a whole host of parameters:

1. Population
   - Reproduction rates (as mediated through social customs)
   - Emergence of new diseases
   - Wars
2. Agricultural production
   - Climate
   - Soil conservation practices
   - Sea farming
   - Genetic engineering
3. Availability of animal foods (sea and land)
4. Conditions of life
   - Quality of life (crime, pollution)
   - Economic conditions (employment)

But each of these items in itself is clearly dependent on further complicated (and sometimes imponderable) factors: each will itself hinge on further estimates that may involve further elements of predictive intractability. Overall, our forecast here very much depends on climate changes, chemical and atomic warfare, the impact of meteorites, and a thousand and one other factors that themselves are difficult if not impossible to foresee. (And matters get even worse when there are cyclical feedback interconnections.) The predictive issue with which we began proceeds to exfoliate into a vast proliferation of others that themselves are similarly complex.

All in all, then, the multitude of difficulties that lie in the way of predictive foresight conspire to make the future, and in particular the sector of it that is of principal concern to us—namely, our own future—into a terra incognita of unavoidable ignorance.[1]

Can Computers Mend Matters?

COULD COMPUTERS OVERCOME OUR LIMITATIONS?

In view of the difficulties and limitations that beset our human efforts at answering the questions we confront in a complex world, it becomes tempting to contemplate the possibility that computers might enable us to overcome our cognitive disabilities and surmount those epistemic frailties of ours. And so we may wonder: Can computers remove our ignorance and overcome our limitations? If a problem is to qualify as solvable at all, will computers always be able to solve it for us?

Of course, computers cannot bear human offspring, enter into contractual agreements, or exhibit heroism. But such processes address *practical* problems relating to the management of the affairs of human life and so do not count in the present cognitive context. Then, too, we must put aside *evaluative* problems of normative bearing or of matters of human affectivity and sensibility: computers cannot offer us meaningful consolation or give advice to the lovelorn. The issue presently at hand regards the capacity of computers to resolve *cognitive* problems of empirical or formal fact. Typically, the sort of problems that will concern us here are those that characterize cognition, in particular problems relating to the description, explanation, and prediction of the things, events, and processes that comprise the realm of physical reality. And to all visible appearances computers are ideal instruments for addressing the matters of cognitive complexity that arise in such contexts. The history of computation in recent times is one of a confident march from triumph to triumph. Time and again, those who have affirmed the limitedness of computers have been forced into ignominious retreat as increasingly powerful machines implementing increasingly ingenious programs have been able to achieve the supposedly unachievable. However, the question now before us is not, "Can computers *help* with problem solving?"—an issue that demands a resounding affirmative and needs little further discussion. There is no doubt whatever that computers can do a lot here—and very possibly more than we ourselves can. But the question before us is "Is there anything in the domain of cognitive problem solving that computers cannot manage to do?" And there is an awesomely wide gap between *much* and *everything*.

First some important preliminaries. To begin with, we must, in this present context, recognize that much more is at issue with a computer than a mere electronic calculating machine understood in terms of its operational hardware. For one thing, software also counts. And, for another, so does data acquisition. As we here construe computers, they are electronic information-managing devices equipped with data banks and augmented with sensors as autonomous data access. Such computers are able not only to *process* information but also to *obtain* it. Moreover, the computers at issue here are, so we shall suppose, capable of discovering and learning, and thereby able significantly to extend and elaborate their own initially programmed modus operandi. Computers in this presently operative sense are not mere calculating machines, but general problem solvers along the lines of the fanciful contraptions envisioned by the aficionados of artificial intelligence. These enhanced computers are accordingly question-answering devices of a very ambitious order.

On this expanded view of the matter, we must correspondingly enlarge our vision both of what computers can do and what can reasonably be asked of them. For it is the potential of computers as an instrumentality for universal problem solving that concerns us here, and not merely their more limited role in the calculations of algorithmic decision theory. The computers at issue will thus be prepared to deal with factually substantive as well as merely formal (logico-mathematical) issues. And this means that the questions we can ask are correspondingly diverse. For here, as elsewhere, added power brings added responsibility. The questions it is appropriate to ask thus can relate not just to matters of calculation but also to the things and processes of the world.

Moreover, some preliminary discussion of the nature of problem solving is required, because one has to become clear from the outset about what it is to *solve* a cognitive problem. Obviously enough, this is a matter of answering questions. Now, to answer a question can be construed in three ways: to offer a *possible* answer, to offer a *correct* answer, and finally to offer a *credible* answer. It is the third of these senses that will be at the center of concern here. And with good reason. For consider a problem solver that proceeds in one of the following ways: it replies "yes" to every yes/no question; or it figures out the range of possible answers and then randomizes to select one; or it proceeds by "pure guesswork." Even though these so-called problem solvers may give the correct response some or much of the time, they are systematically unable to resolve our questions in the presently operative credibility-oriented sense of the term. For the obviously sensible stance calls for holding that *a cognitive problem is resolved only when a correct answer is convincingly provided*—that is to say, when we have a solution that we can responsibly accept and acknowledge as such. Resolving a problem is not just a matter of having an answer, and not even of having an answer that happens to be correct. The actual resolution of a problem must be credible and convincing—with the answer provided in such a way that its cogency is recognizable. In general problem solving we want not just a response but an *answer*—a resolution equipped with a contextual rationale to establish its credibility in a way accessible to duly competent recipients. To be warranted in accepting a third-party answer we must ourselves have case-specific reasons to acknowledge it as correct. A response whose appropriateness as such cannot secure rational confidence is no answer at all.[1] And in this regard we are in the driver's seat because in seeking acceptable answers for computers we are bound to mean *acceptable to us.*

With these crucial preliminaries out of the way, we are ready to begin.

GENERAL-PRINCIPLE LIMITS ARE NOT MEANINGFUL LIMITATIONS

The question before us is, "Are there *any* significant cognitive problems that computers cannot solve?" Now it must be acknowledged from the outset that certain problems are inherently unsolvable in the logical nature of things. One cannot square the circle. One cannot co-measure the incommensurable. One cannot decide the demonstrably undecidable nor prove the demonstrably unprovable. Such tasks represent absolute limitations whose accomplishment is theoretically impossible—unachievable for reasons of general principle rooted in the nature of the realities at issue.[2] And it is clear that inherently unsolvable problems cannot be solved by computers either.[3]

Other sorts of problems will not be unsolvable as such, but will, nevertheless, be demonstrably proven to be computationally intractable. For with respect to *purely theoretical* problems it is clear from Turingesque results in algorithmic decision theory that there will indeed be computer insolubilia—mathematical questions to which an algorithmic respondent will give the wrong answer or be unable to give any answers at all, no matter how much time is allowed.[4] But this is a mathematical fact that obtains of necessity so that this whole issue can be also set aside for present purposes. For in the present context of universal problem solving, the necessitarian facts of Gödel-Church-Turing incompleteness become irrelevant. Here any search for *meaningful* problem-solving limitations will have to confine its attention to problems that are in principle solvable: *demonstrably* unsolvable problems are beside the point of present concern because an inability to do what is in principle impossible hardly qualifies as a limitation, seeing that it makes no sense to ask for the demonstrably impossible.

For present purposes, then, it is limits of *capability,* not limits of *feasibility,* that matter. In asking about the problem-solving limitedness of computers, we are looking to problems that *computers* cannot resolve but that other problem solvers conceivably can. The limits that will concern us here are accordingly not rooted in conceptual or logico-mathematical infeasibilities of general principle nor in absolute physical impossibilities, but rather in performatory limitations imposed specifically upon computers by the world's contingent *modus operandi.*

And in this formulation the adverb "specifically" does real work by way of ruling out certain computer limitations as irrelevant. Thus some problems will simply be too large given the inevitable limitations on computers in terms of memory, size, processing time, and output capacity. Suppose for the moment that we inhabit a universe which, while indeed boundless, is nevertheless finite. No computer could possibly solve a problem whose output requires printing more letters or numbers than there are atoms in the universe. However, such problems ask computers to achieve a task that is not "substantively meaningful" in the sense that no physical agent at all—computer, organism, or whatever—could possibly achieve it. By contrast, the problems that concern us here are those that are not solution-precluding on the basis of inherent mathematical or physical impossibilities. To reemphasize: our concern is with the performative limitations of computers with regard to problems that are not inherently intractable in the logical or physical nature of things. It is on this basis that we must proceed here.

PRACTICAL LIMITS: INADEQUATE INFORMATION

Often the information needed for credible problem resolution is simply unavailable. Thus no problem solver can at this point in time provide credible answers to questions such as, "What did Julius Caesar have for breakfast on that fatal Ides of March?" or "Who will be the first auto accident victim of the next millennium?" The information needed to answer such questions is just not available at this stage. In all problem-solving situations, the performance of computers is decisively limited by the quality of the information at their disposal. "Garbage in, garbage out," as the saying has it. But matters are in fact worse than this. Garbage can come out even where no garbage goes in.

One clear example of the practical limits of computer problem solving arises in the context of prediction. Consider the two prediction problems set out in display 7.1.

On first sight, there seems to be little difficulty in arriving at a prediction in these cases. But now suppose that we acquire some further data to enlarge our background information: pieces of information supplementary to—but nowise conflicting with or corrective of—the given premises:

Display 7.1. Prediction problems

Case 1

Data: *X* is confronted with the choice of reading a novel by Dickens or one by Trollope. And further: *X* is fond of Dickens.

Problem: To predict which novel *X* will read.

Case 2

Data: *Z* has just exactly ten dollars. And further: *Z* promised to repay his neighbor seven dollars today. Moreover, *Z* is a thoroughly honest individual.

Problem: To predict what *Z* will do with his money.

Case 1: *X* is extremely, indeed *inordinately*, fond of Trollope.

Case 2: *Z* also promised to repay his other neighbor the seven dollars he borrowed on the same occasion.

Note that in each case our initial information is nowise abrogated but merely enlarged by the additions in question. But nevertheless in each case we are impelled, in the light of that supplementation, to *change* the response we were initially prepared and rationally well-advised to make. Thus when I know nothing further of next year's Fourth of July parade in Centerville U.S.A., I shall predict that its music will be provided by a marching band; but if I am additionally informed that the Loyal Sons of Old Hibernia have been asked to provide the music, then bagpipes will now come to the fore.

It must, accordingly, be recognized that the search for rationally appropriate answers to certain questions can be led astray not just by the *incorrectness* of information but by its *incompleteness* as well. The specific body of information that is actually at hand is not just important for problem resolution, it is *crucial*. And we can never be unalloyedly confident of problem resolutions based on incomplete information, seeing that further information can always come along to upset the applecart. As available information expands, established problem resolutions can always become destabilized. One crucial practical limitation of computers in matters of problem solving is thus constituted by the inevitable incompleteness (to say nothing of potential incorrectness) of the information at their disposal. And here the fact that computers can only ever ingest finite—and thus incomplete—bodies of information means that their problem-resolving performance is always at risk. Computers are physical devices; they are subject to the laws of physics and limited by the realities of the physical universe. In particular, since a computer can process no more than a fixed number of bits per second per gram, the potential complexity of algorithms means that there is only so much that a given computer can possibly manage to do.

Then there is also the temporal aspect. To solve problems about the real world, a computer must of course be equipped with information about it. But securing and processing information is a time-consuming process, and the time at issue can never be reduced to an instantaneous zero. Time-constrained problems that are enormously complex—those whose solution calls for securing and processing a vast amount of data—can exceed the reach for any computer. At some point it always becomes impossible to squeeze the needed operations into available time. There are only so many numbers that a computer can crunch in a given day. And so if the problem is a predictive one it could find itself in the awkward position that it should have started yesterday on a problem only presented to it today. Thus even under the (fact-contravening) supposition that the computer can answer *all* of our questions, it cannot, if we are impatient enough, produce those answers as promptly as we might require them. Even when given, answers may be given too late.

This situation is emblematic of a larger issue. Any computer that we humans can possibly contrive is going to be finite: its sensors will be finite, its memory (however large) will be finite, and its processing time (however fast) will be finite.[5] Moreover, computers operate in a context of finite instructions and finite inputs. Any representational model that functions by means of computers is of finite complexity in this sense. It is always a finitely characterizable system: its descriptive constitution is characterized in many finite information-specifying steps, and its operations are always ultimately presented by many finite instructions. And this array of finitudes means that a computer's modeling of the real will never capture the inherent ramifications of the natural universe of which it itself is a constituent (albeit a minute one). Artifice cannot replicate the complexity of the real; reality is richer in its descriptive constitution and more efficient in its transformatory processes than human artifice can ever manage to realize. For nature itself has a complexity that is effectively endless, so that no finistic model that purports to represent nature can ever replicate the detail of reality's makeup in a fully comprehensive way, even as no architect's blueprint-plus-specifications can possibly specify *every* feature of the structure that is ultimately erected. In particular, the complications of a continuous universe cannot be captured completely via the resources of discretized computer languages. All endeavors to represent reality—computer models emphatically included—involve some element of oversimplification, and in general a great deal of it.

The fact of the matter is that reality is too complex for adequate cognitive manipulation. Cognitive friction always enters into matters of information management. Our cognitive processing is never totally efficient. Something is always lost in the process. Cognitive entropy is always upon the scene. But as far as knowledge is concerned, nature does nothing in vain and so encompasses no altogether irrelevant detail. Yet oversimplification always makes for losses, for deficiencies in cognition. For representational omissions are never totally irrelevant, so that no oversimplified descriptive model can get the full range of predictive and explanatory matters exactly right. Put figuratively, it could be said that the only "computer" that can keep pace with reality's twists and turns over time is the universe itself. It would be unreasonable to expect any computer model less complex than this totality itself to provide a fully adequate representation of it, in particular because that computer model must of course itself be incorporated *within* the universe.

PERFORMATIVE LIMITS OF PREDICTION—SELF-INSIGHT OBSTACLES

Another important sort of practical limitation to computer problem solving arises not from the inherent intractability of questions but from their unsuitability for particular respondents. Specifically, one of the issues regarding which a computer can never function perfectly is its own predictive performance. One critical respect in which the self-insight of computers is limited arises in connection with what is known as "the halting problem" in algorithmic decision theory. Even if a problem is computer solvable—in the sense that a suitable computer will demonstrably be able to find a solution by keeping at it long enough—it will in general be impossible to foretell how long a process of calculation will actually be needed. There is not—and demonstrably cannot be—a *general* procedure for foretelling with respect to a particular computer and a particular problem: "Here is how long it will take to find the solution—and if the problem is not solved within this time span then it is not solvable at all." No computer can provide general insight into how long it—or any other computer, for that matter—will take to solve problems. The question, "How long is long enough?" demonstrably admits of no general solution here. And computers are—of necessity!—bound to fail even in much simpler self-predictive matters. Thus consider confronting a predictor with the problem posed by the question:

P_1: *When next you answer a question, will the answer be*
   negative?

This is a question that—for reasons of general principle—no predictor can ever answer satisfactorily.[6] For consider the available possibilities:

Answer given	Actually correct answer	Agreement?
Yes	No	No
No	Yes	No
Can't say	No	No

On this question, there just is no way in which a predictive computer's response could possibly agree with the actual fact of the matter. Even the seemingly plausible response "I can't say" automatically constitutes a self-falsifying answer, since in giving this answer the predictor would automatically make "No" into the response called for by the proprieties of the situation.

Here, then, we have a question that will inevitably confound any conscientious predictor and drive it into baffled perplexity. But of course the problem poses a perfectly meaningful question to which *another* predictor could give a putatively correct answer—namely, by saying, "No, that predictor cannot answer this question at all; the question will condemn a predictor (Predictor No. 1) to baffled silence." But of course the answer, "I am responding with baffled silence," is one which that initial predictor cannot cogently offer. And as to that baffled silence itself, this is something which, as such, would clearly constitute a defeat for Predictor No. 1. Still, that question which impelled Predictor No. 1 into perplexity and unavoidable failure presents no problem of principle for Predictor No. 2. And this clearly shows that there is nothing improper about that question as such. For while the question posed in P_1 will be irresolvable by a *particular* computer, and so it could—in theory—be answered by *other* computers is not irresolvable by computers in general. However, there are other questions that indeed are computer insolubilia for computers at large. One of them is the following:

> P_2: What is an example of a predictive question that no computer will ever state?

In answering *this* question the computer would have to stake a claim of the form "Q is an example of a predictive question that no computer will ever state." And in the very making of this claim the computer would falsify it. It is thus automatically unable to effect a satisfactory resolution. However, the question is neither meaningless nor irresolvable. A *noncomputer* problem solver could in theory answer it correctly. Its presupposition, "There is a predictive question that no computer will ever consider," is beyond doubt true. What we thus have in P_2 is an example of an in-principle solvable—and thus "meaningful"—question that, as a matter of necessity in the logical scheme of things, no problem-solving computer can ever resolve satisfactorily. The long and short of it is that every predictor—computers included—is bound to manifest versatility-incapacities with respect to its own predictive operations.[7]

However, from the angle of our present considerations, the shortcoming of problems P_1 and of P_2 is that they are computer irresolvable on the basis of theoretical general principles. And it is therefore not appropriate, on the present perspective—as explained above—to count this sort of thing as a computer limitation. Are there any other, less problematic examples?

PERFORMATIVE LIMITS: A DEEPER LOOK

At this point we must contemplate some fundamental realities of the situation confronting our problem-solving resources. The first of these is that no computer can ever reliably determine that all its more powerful compeers are unable to resolve a particular substantive problem (that is, one that is inherently tractable and not demonstrably unsolvable on logico-conceptual grounds). And in view of the theoretical possibility of ever more powerful computers, this means the following:

T_1: *No computer can reliably determine that a given substantive problem is altogether computer irresolvable.*

Moreover, something that we are not prepared to accept from any computer is cognitive megalomania. No computer is, we may safely suppose, ever able to achieve credibility in staking a claim to the effect that no substantive problem whatever is beyond the capacity reach of computers. And this leads to the following thesis:

T_2: *No computer can reliably determine that all substantive problems whatever are computer resolvable.*

But just what is the ultimate rationale for these theses?

A COMPUTER INSOLUBILIUM

The time has come to turn from generalities to specifics. At this point we can confront a problem-solving computer with the challenging question:

P_3: *What is an example of a (substantive) problem that no computer whatsoever can resolve?*

There are three possibilities here:

1. The computer offers an answer of the format "P is an example of a problem that no computer whatsoever can resolve." For reasons already canvassed we would not see this as an acceptable resolution, since by T_1 our respondent cannot achieve credibility here.

2. The computer responds: "No can do: I am unable to resolve this problem: it lies outside my capability." We could—and would—accept this response and take our computer at its word. But the response of course represents no more than computer acquiescence in computer incapability.

3. The computer responds: "I reject the question as improper and illegitimate on the grounds of its being based on an inappropriate presupposition, namely that there are indeed problems that no computer whatsoever can resolve." We ourselves would have to reject this position as inappropriate in the face of T_2. The response at issue here is one that we would simply be unable to accept at face value from a computer.

It follows from such deliberations that P_3 is itself a problem that no computer can resolve satisfactorily.

At this point, then, we have realized the principal object of the discussion: We have been able to identify a meaningful concrete problem that is computer irresolvable for reasons that are embedded—via theses T_1 and T_2—in the world's empirical realities. For—to reemphasize—our present concern is with issues of general problem solving and not algorithmic decision theory.

To this point, however, our discussion has not, as yet, entered the doctrinal terrain of discussions along the lines of Hubert L. Dreyfus's *What Computers Still Can't Do.*[8] The project there is to compare computer information processing with human performance to show that there are things that humans can do that computers cannot. However, the present discussion has to this point looked solely to problems that computers cannot manage to resolve. Whether *humans* can or cannot resolve them has remained out of sight.

The big question that remains untouched is this: Is there any sector of this problem-solving domain where the human mind enjoys a competitive advantage over computers? Specifically:

P_4: *Are there problems that computers cannot solve satisfactorily but people can?*

And in fact what we would ideally like to have is not just an abstract answer to P_4, but a concrete answer to the following:

P_5: *What is an example of a problem that computers cannot solve satisfactorily but people can?*

What we are now seeking is a computer-defeating question that has the three characteristics of posing a meaningful problem, being computer-unsolvable, and admitting of a viable resolution by intelligent noncomputers, specifically humans.[9]

This is what we are looking for. And—lo and behold!—*we have already found it.* All we need do is to turn around and look back to P_3. After all, P_3 is—so it was argued—a problem that computers cannot resolve satisfactorily, and this consideration automatically provides us—people that we are—with the example that is being asked for. In presenting P_3 within its present context we have in fact resolved it. And, moreover, P_5 is itself also a problem of just this same sort. It, too, is a computer-unresolvable question that people can manage to resolve.[10]

In the end, then, the ironic fact remains that the very question we are considering regarding cognitive problems that computers cannot solve but people can provides its own answer.[11] P_3 and P_5 appear to be eligible for membership in the category of "academic questions"— questions that are effectively self-resolving—a category that also includes such prosaic members as "What is an example of a question formulated in English?" and "What is an example of a question that asks for an example of something?" The presently operative mode of computer unsolvability thus pivots on the factor of self-reference— just as is the case with Gödelian incompleteness.

To be sure, their inability to answer the question, "What is a question that no computer can possibly resolve?" is—viewed in a suitably formidable perspective—a token of the power of computers rather than of their limitedness. After all, we see the person who maintains "I can't think of something I can't accomplish" not as unimaginative but as a megalomaniac—and one who uses "we" instead of "I" as only slightly less so. But nevertheless, in the present case this pretension to strength marks a point of weakness.

The key issue is whether computers might be defeated by questions that other problem solvers, such as humans, could overcome. The preceding deliberations indicate that there indeed are such limitations. For the ramifications of self-reference are such that no computer could satisfactorily answer certain questions regarding the limitation of the general capacity of computers to solve questions. But humans can in fact resolve such questions because, with them, no self-reference is involved.

But could not a computer simply follow in the wake of our own reasoning here and instance P_3 and P_5 as self-resolving? Not really. For in view of the considerations adduced in relation to T_1–T_2 above, a computer cannot convincingly monitor the range of computer-tractable problems. And so the responses of a computer in this sort of issue simply could not secure rational conviction.

RETROSPECT

The key lesson of these deliberations is thus clear: computers can reduce but not eliminate our cognitive limitation. However much computers may surpass us in capacity, the fact remains that the same sorts of limitations that mark us as finite knowers will afflict computers as well. Computers can no more annihilate our cognitive limitations than machines can eliminate our physical limitations.

And the matter has yet another aspect. It has to be realized that computers are our instruments and not our replacements. To accept something as true is always a matter of acting on one's own responsibility. When one endorses something on the basis of another's say-so—be it another person, or a reference source, or a computer auxiliary—the fact remains that the responsibility for so proceeding lies on one's own shoulders. In accepting p on the basis of X's say-so I not only commit myself to p but to X's veracity and reliability as well. In matters relating to p I may well trust your judgment more than mine. But if I do not trust my judgment in matters of your reliability, your views on p will not help me in settling the issue. And here it does not matter whether you are a person or a computer. In the final analysis, the use of computers is no panacea for cognitive debility, for where there is no self-trust at all computers cannot be of aid.[12]

Implications of
Ignorance

PRELIMINARIES

The preceding deliberations have brought to light a considerable variety of types of fact that, on the basis of general principles, are bound to be unknown or even unknowable. The categories at issue here are first and foremost the following:

- Certain facts regarding our own ignorance
- Certain facts whose determination requires inaccessible data or impracticable measurements
- Certain facts involving information hidden in a statistical fog
- Certain facts deliberately kept secret by others
- Certain facts about the past that have left no trace
- Certain facts regarding the detail of future discoveries

- Certain facts regarding future contingencies
- Certain facts involving vagrant predicates
- Certain facts involving superior intelligences

The basic principle that renders various types of fact unknowable are ultimately of two sorts: (1) those inherent in the contingencies of the world's ways, and (2) those inherent in logico-conceptual considerations. Display 8.1 elaborates this distinction in greater detail.

Our ignorance is sometimes grounded in operations of nature that render certain fact-determinations impossible in the circumstances, and it is sometimes grounded in the insufficiency of our information-accessing resources. But more interesting yet are those cases of necessary ignorance where knowledge becomes unrealizable on logico-conceptual grounds—self-reflexive unknowing, predictive vagrancy, and intellectual disparity.

Display 8.1. Grounds of ignorance

- Contingent ignorance

    Ontologically grounded: rooted in nature's modus operandi

    - Interventions of chance (How will the coin toss eventuate?)
    - Machinations of chaos (How will the smoke drifts dissipate?)
    - Trace erasure (Just what were sand dunes or cloud formations of a year ago?)

    Epistemically grounded: rooted in the inadequacy of our information securing resources

    - Inaccessibility of required data (What did Caesar have for breakfast on that fatal Ides of March?)
    - Inadequacy of observational resources (Just how many grains of sand are there in the Sahara desert?)

- Necessary ignorance

    - Regarding the detail of our own ignorance
    - Regarding matters involving vagrant predicates
    - Regarding the working of superior intelligences

THE VAGARIES OF VAGUENESS

While the present deliberations are focused upon ignorance, they nevertheless provide no basis for a radical scepticism. For they do not take the pessimistic line of a cognitive negativism to the effect that knowledge about the world is unachievable. On the contrary, the present approach is one of cautious optimism, arguing that while reliable information is often not as readily achievable as people are inclined to think, the cognitive enterprise nevertheless can successfully come to terms with this fact. Evolutionary considerations afford us good reason to think that we exist in a user-friendly world where we need not be right about things for opinion-guided action to be successful. And indeed even in cognitive matters we can—strange to say—manage to extract truth from error. Let us see how this comes to be.

One fundamental feature of inquiry is represented by the following observation:

> Thesis 1: *Insofar as our thinking is vague, truth is accessible even in the face of ignorance.*

Consider the situation where you correctly accept *P*-or-*Q*. But—so let it be supposed—the truth of this disjunction roots entirely in that of *P*, while *Q* is of otherwise undetermined truth status. However, you accept *P*-or-*Q* only because you are convinced of the truth of *Q*, whereas *P* is something about which you have no information at all. Nevertheless, despite your ignorance, your belief is entirely true and appropriate.[1] This example illustrates a far-reaching point.

> Thesis 2: *There is in general an inverse relationship between the precision or definiteness of a judgment and its security: detail and reliability stand in a competing relationship.*

Increased confidence in the correctness of our estimates can always be purchased at the price of decreased accuracy. We estimate the height of the tree at *around* 25 feet. We are *quite sure* that the tree is 25±5 feet high. We are *virtually certain* that its height is 25±10 feet. But we can be *completely and absolutely sure* that its height is between 1 inch and 100 yards. Of this we can be "completely sure" in the sense that we are "absolutely certain," "certain beyond the shadow of a doubt," "as certain as we can be of anything in the world," "so sure that we would be willing to stake our life on it," and the like. For any sort of estimate whatsoever, there is always a characteristic trade-off relationship between the evidential *security* of the estimate, on the one hand (as determinable on the basis of its probability or degree of acceptability), and, on the other hand, its contextual *definitiveness* (exactness, detail, precision, etc.). The situation that obtains is depicted in the curve of display 8.2, with the result that a *complementarity* relationship of sorts holds between definiteness and security.[2]

This state of affairs has far-reaching consequences. It suggests, in particular, that no secure generalization about reality can say exactly

---

Display 8.2. The trade-off between security and definiteness in estimation

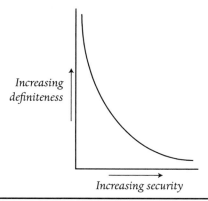

Increasing definiteness

Increasing security

Note: Given suitable ways of measuring security (s) and definitiveness (d), the curve at issue can be supposed to be the equilateral hyperbola: $s \times d =$ constant.

how matters of real significance stand universally—always and everywhere. To capture the real fact of things by means of language we must proceed by way of "warranted approximation." We can be reasonably sure of how things "usually" are and how they "roughly" are, but not of how they always and exactly are.

The moral of this story is that, insofar as our ignorance of relevant matters leads us to be vague in our judgments, we may well manage to enhance our chances of being right. The fact of the matter is that we have:

> Thesis 3: *By constraining us to make vaguer judgments, ignorance enhances our access to correct information (albeit at the cost of less detail and precision).*

Thus if I have forgotten that Seattle is in Washington State, then if "forced to guess" I might well erroneously locate it in Oregon. Nevertheless, my vague judgment that "Seattle is located in the Pacific Northwest" is quite correct. This state of affairs means that when the truth of our claims is critical, we generally play it safe and make our commitments less definite and detailed. Vagueness clearly provides a protective shell that helps to safeguard a statement against falsity. Irrespective of how matters might actually stand within a vast range of alternative circumstances and conditions, the statement remains secure, its truth unaffected by which possibility is realized. And in practical matters, in particular, such rough guidance is often altogether enough. We need not know just exactly how much rain there will be to make it sensible for us to take an umbrella.

COGNITIVE RISK AND THE DEFICITS OF SCEPTICISM

In view of the preceding consideration we also have the following:

> Thesis 4: *In practice our beliefs are often overdetermined by the evidence. In order to be sure, we generally "overdesign" our beliefs*

in matters that are important to us by keeping them comparatively indefinite.

Engineers standardly overdesign their productions. They build the bridge to bear more weight than will ever be placed upon it; they build the dam to withstand far more pressure than the reservoir is expected to exert. Analogously, our beliefs will—especially in matters of importance—generally be such that the relevant evidence at our disposal would actually support something far stronger. Whenever error-avoidance is a significant issue, we form our beliefs so guardedly that the evidence at our disposal would even support stronger and more content-laden claims. In the face of our cognitive shortcomings, we overdesign our claims to knowledge.

All the same, it is clear that risk avoidance in matters of belief stands coordinate with scepticism. The sceptic's line is: Run no risk of error; take no chances with falsehood; accept nothing that does not come with totally ironclad guarantees. And the proviso here is largely academic, seeing that little if anything in this world comes with absolutely ironclad guarantees—certainly nothing by way of interesting knowledge. It must, however, be recognized that in general two fundamentally different kinds of misfortunes can arise in cognitive situations where risks are run and chances taken:

1. Omission errors: We fail to accept something which, as it turns out, we should have accepted. We decline to take the chance, we avoid running the risk at issue, but things turn out favorably after all, so that we lose the gamble.

2. Commission errors: We accept something which, as it turns out, we should have rejected. We do take the chance and run the risk at issue, but things go wrong, so that we lose the gamble.

Display 8.3. The cost of risk-management approaches

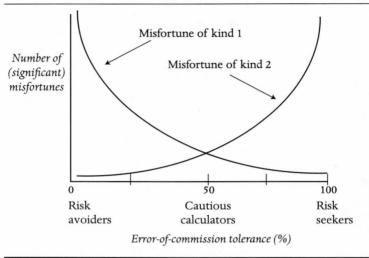

If we are risk seekers, we will incur few misfortunes of the first kind, but, things being what they are, many of the second kind will befall us. On the other hand, if we are risk avoiders, we shall suffer few misfortunes of the second kind but shall inevitably incur many of the first. In cognitive matters, ignorance is the inevitable price of over-caution. (The situation has the general structure depicted in display 8.3.)

Clearly, the reasonable thing to do is to adopt a policy that minimizes misfortunes overall. And this means that a rigid policy of avoiding all errors of a given type (be it omission or commission) will, in general, fail to be rationally optimal. Both approaches engender too many misfortunes for comfort. The sensible and prudent thing is to adopt the middle-of-the-road policy of risk calculation, striving as best we can to balance the positive risks of outright loss against the negative ones of lost opportunity. The rule of reason calls for sensible management and a prudent calculation of risks; it standardly enjoins upon us the Aristotelian golden mean between extremes of gullibility and ignorance.

Turning now to the specifically cognitive case, it may be observed that the sceptic succeeds splendidly in averting misfortunes of the second kind. He makes no errors of commission; by accepting nothing, he accepts nothing false. But, of course, he loses out on the opportunity to obtain information. He avoids falsity at the price of ignorance. The sceptic thus errs on the side of safety. By contrast, there is the overly uncautious, gullible believer. Such an individual will not have many questions unanswered, but does this at the expense of incurring errors of commission. The sensible course is clearly that of a prudent calculation of risks.

Ultimately, we face a question of trade-offs. Are we prepared to run a greater risk of mistakes to secure the potential benefit of an enlarged understanding? In the end, the matter is one of priorities—of safety as against information and of an epistemological risk aversion as against the impetus to understanding. The ultimate issue is one of values and priorities, weighing the negativity of ignorance and incomprehension against the risk of mistakes and misinformation. Safety engineering in inquiry is like safety engineering in life. There must be proper balance between costs and benefits.

All the same there is only so much that we can do by way of controlling cognitive mishaps. We live in a world without easy options—and without guarantees.

FULLER INFORMATION DOES NOT GUARANTEE SAFETY

One of the deepest ironies of the epistemic realm is represented by the following:

Thesis 5: *It would be an error to think that a conclusion based on fuller information is necessarily an improvement, presenting us with a result that cannot be false if its "inferior" predecessor was already true.*

If the contention at issue were indeed true, then as more information is added, an outcome's claims on truth would align even more closely to the volume of evidence, and could not—as is potentially so—oscillate between increases and decreases in plausibility or probability. But this is clearly not so.

Consider the following example, based on the question, "What will John do to occupy himself on the trip?" Suppose we require an answer to this question. But suppose further that the following data become successively available:

1. He loves doing crosswords.

2. He loves reading mysteries even more.

3. He didn't take any books along.

It is clear that we are led to and fro. Initially (at stage 1 of information access) we incline to the answer that he will be working crosswords. At the next stage, when item 2 arrives, we change our mind and incline to the answer that he will be reading. With item 3 we abandon this idea and go back to our initial view. And of course a subsequent stage, say one where we have

4. One of this fellow passengers lends him a book.

can nevertheless reverse the situation and return matters to step 2. And who knows what step 5 will bring? The crucial point is that additional information need not serve to settle matters by bringing us closer to the truth, and that a conclusion based on fuller knowledge is not thereby automatically more likely to be correct.

Throughout the realm of inductive or plausible reasoning, P and Q can always point to a conclusion at odds with that indicated by

F alone: the circumstance that fact P renders X highly probable is wholly compatible with the existence of another fact Q of such a sort that P & Q renders X highly improbable. And yet what Q undermines here can always be restored by some yet further additional fact.

Such situations are called nonmonotonic because additional knowledge always has the potential of constraining a change of mind—rather than merely providing additional substantiation for a fixed result. We have no assurance that further information produces a closer approximation to the truth. Additional information can serve to skew yet further an already biased picture. It can—all too easily—point perfectly sensible and rational people to the wrong conclusion even when proceeding by perfectly sensible and rational courses of inference. Accordingly, there are bound to be many sorts of situations in which people are better off without various items of knowledge—better off in ignorance, so to speak. Conclusions based on additional information may in some sense be comparatively "better" or "securer" but they need certainly not be "truer" or "more accurate." There is a series in which additional information does not reduce ignorance.

And, in fact, ignorance can have its compensations. While it is certainly not the purpose of the present discussion to provide an essay "In Praise of Ignorance," nevertheless the reality of it is that the dictum that "ignorance is bliss" is not invariably inappropriate. There is a natural tendency—among intellectuals in particular—to think of knowledge as an invariably good thing. Ironically, however, the awkward fact that additional knowledge can be counterproductive and misleading is something that one just cannot ignore.[3]

In this imperfect world, we are not generally in a position to achieve the absolute best as such, but have to settle for the best *available* (or *discernible*) reason. We have to content ourselves with doing "the *apparently* best thing"—the best that we can manage in the prevailing circumstances. But the fact remains that what is rationally optimal need not be correct. Things can all too easily go wrong here. The problem about doing the rational thing—doing that which we sensibly suppose to be supported by the best reasons—is that we realize full well that our information, inevitably being incomplete, may well point us in the wrong direction. We can never secure advance guarantees that what we do not know makes no difference. The impact of ignorance is beyond the possibility of prejudgment.

IGNORANCE BETOKENS REALISM

It is one of the most fundamental aspects of our concept of a real thing that our knowledge of it is imperfect—that the reality of something actual—any bit of concrete existence—is such as to transcend what we can know since there is always more to be said about it. And the inescapable fact of fallibilism and limitedness—of our absolute confidence that our putative knowledge does *not* do justice to the truth of the matter of what reality is actually like—is surely one of the best arguments for a realism. After all, the truth and nothing but the truth is one thing, but the *whole* truth is something else again. And if a comprehensively adequately grasp of "the way things really are" is beyond our powers, then this very circumstance itself constitutes a strong ground for a conviction that there is more to reality than we humans do or can know about.

In particular, the world's descriptive complexity is literally limitless. For it is clear that the number of true descriptive remarks that can be made about a thing—about any concrete element of existence, and, in specific, any particular physical object—is theoretically inexhaustible. Take a stone, for example. Consider its physical features: its shape, its surface texture, its chemistry, etc. And then consider its causal background: its genesis and subsequent history. And then consider its functional aspects as reflected in its uses by the stonemason, or the architect, or the landscape decorator, etc. There is, in principle, no end to the different lines of consideration available to yield descriptive truths, so that the totality of potentially available facts about a thing—about any real thing whatever—is bottomless. John Maynard Keynes's "Principle of Limited Variety" is simply wrong: there is no inherent limit to the number of distinct descriptive kinds or categories to which the things of this world can belong. Who can ever say that there is not more to be said about something within nature's panoply of reals? As best we can possibly tell, natural reality has an infinite descriptive depth. It confronts us with a Law of Natural Complexity: *There is in principle no limit to the number of natural kinds to which any concrete particular belongs.*[4] And this of course means that reality has a cognitive profundity whose bottom we can never hope to fathom altogether.

The world's things are cognitively opaque: we cannot see through to the bottom of them. And this is something about which, in principle, we cannot delude ourselves, since such delusion would vindicate rather than deny a reality of facts independent of ourselves. It is the very limitation of our knowledge of things—our recognition that reality extends beyond the horizons of what we can possibly know about it—that perhaps best betokens the mind-transcendence of the real. The very inadequacy of our knowledge militates toward philosophical realism, because it clearly betokens that there is a reality out there that lies beyond the inadequate gropings of mind. Ignorance by nature requires a real factuality to be ignorant about.

One of the positive consequences of unavoidable ignorance is that it facilitates life being a voyage to discovery. If ignorance were extinguished and everything knowable known, open horizons would be replaced by a walled enclosure. Important facets of life's mystery and excitement would be lost forever. And so in the end ignorance is not an unalloyed negativity—even apart from its role as a goad to the virtue of humility.

NOTES

PREFACE

1. Plato, *Apology*, 20E–23B.

2. On these issues see the author's *Scepticism: A Critical Reappraisal* (Oxford: Basil Blackwell, 1980).

3. Diogenes Laertius, *Lives of the Philosophers*, II:32.

CHAPTER 1. THE REACH OF IGNORANCE

1. Thomas Jefferson, *Notes in the State of Virginia*.

2. The difference between unknown and unknowable facts is most clearly expressed in symbolic terms. A fact is unknowable when:

$$\sim\Diamond(\exists x)Kxf \text{ or equivalently } \Box(\forall x)\sim Kxf$$

By contrast a fact is merely unknown but not unknowable when

$$\sim(\exists x)Kxf \,\&\, \Diamond\,(\exists x)Kxf \text{ or equivalently } (\forall x)\sim Kxf \,\&\, \Diamond(\exists x)Kxf$$

3. If I am to claim that f is a fact that nobody knows, then I affirm

1. $Ki(f \,\&\, \sim(\exists x)Kxf)$

where i = oneself. Now since $Kx(p \,\&\, q)$ entails $Kxp \,\&\, Kxq$, 1 entails

2. $Kif \,\&\, \sim Ki\sim(\exists x)Kxy$

But since Kxp entails p, 2 entails

3. $Kif \,\&\, \sim(\exists x)Kxf$

And this thesis is self-contradictory. I can unproblematically claim that there are unknown facts but cannot possibly adduce a specific example of one.

The best one can ever do to be specific here is to give examples of unanswerable questions.

4. The former comes down to maintaining :

$\sim Kip \;\&\; \sim Ki\sim p \quad (i = \text{oneself})$

No problem there: I neither know that p nor that not-p. However, the second statement, to the effect that p is a fact that one does not know to be so, comes down to maintaining $p \;\&\; \sim Kip$. But in claiming to know this, namely

$Ki(p \;\&\; \sim Kip)$

I claim to know (among other things) both that p is true and that I do not know this. And such a claim is self-contradictory.

5. In claiming to know $p \;\&\; \sim Kip$ we claim:

Ki(p $\&$ $\sim$Kip)

But since $Kx(p \;\&\; q) \rightarrow (Kxp \;\&\; Kxq)$ obtains, we obtain both Kip and $Ki(\sim Kip)$. But the latter of these entails $\sim Kip$. And so a manifest contradiction results.

6. Symbolically we have $K(\exists x)Sx$ but emphatically not $(\exists x)KSx$. That quantifier placement makes all the difference.

7. For further details regarding presumptions, see the author's book of this title (Cambridge: Cambridge University Press, 2006).

8. The discussion of this section draws on Chapter 6 of the author's *A Useful Inheritance* (Savage, Md.: Rowman & Littlefield, 1990).

9. It may be thought that there is something incongruous in asking for an evolutionary explanation for something that has not happened. But the issue is rather one of using basic principles of natural process to explain why evolution does not take certain routes. In this regard, the situation with respect to intelligence (i.e., cognitive agility) is not dissimilar from that with regard to motion (i.e., physical agility). Explaining why evolution has not produced a hyperintelligent mammal is structurally akin to explaining why it has not produced a hyperswift one by

outfitting creatures with organic wheels. For an interesting treatment of this issue, see Jared Diamond, "The Biology of the Wheel," *Nature* 302 (April 1983): 572–73.

10. On this issue, compare J.B.S. Haldane's insightful and provocative essay "On Being the Right Size," in his collection *Possible Worlds and Other Papers* (New York: Harper and Brothers, 1927).

11. Of course here—as elsewhere—we cannot let matters rest with speaking of an evolutionary process in this rather anthropomorphic way. In the final analysis, we have to cash in these metaphors in terms of different groups (tribes, clans) of humanoids chancing to produce a bumper crop of more than ordinarily intelligent individuals and finding themselves at a reproductive disadvantage because of their comparatively greater risk-aversiveness. No imaginative student of recent demographic phenomena will find difficulty in envisioning an appropriate sort of scenario here.

12. Thomas Gray, "Ode on a Prospect of Eton College" (1742), ll. 98–99.

13. The author's *Epistemic Logic* (Pittsburgh: University of Pittsburgh Press, 2005), also deals with some themes relevant to this chapter's deliberations.

14. James Ferrier, *Institute of Metaphysics* (Bristol: Thoemones Press, 2001). See the discussion in Jenny Keefe, "James Ferrier and the Theory of Ignorance," *Monist* 90 (2007): 297–309.

15. Ferrier, *Institutes*, 414.

CHAPTER 2. QUESTIONS AND INSOLUBILIA

1. Specifically, the former thesis comes to $(\exists Q)(\sim AxQ)$, while the latter comes to $\sim AxQ$, where x is some individual or other and AxQ abbreviates "x can answer Q."

2. Immanuel Kant, *Prolegomena to Any Future Metaphysic* (1783), sect. 57; *Akad.*, 352.

3. Kant, *Prolegomena*, sect. 57.

4. Some of the issues of this chapter are addressed more elaborately

in the author's *Epistemetrics* (Cambridge: Cambridge University Press, 2005).

5. We have the true $K(\exists x)Fx$ but certainly not the false $(\exists x)KFx$. So the former obtains despite $\sim(\exists x)KFx$.

6. We can, of course, refer to such individuals, and even to some extent describe them. But what we cannot do is *identify* them in the sense specified above.

7. Accordingly, we have $K(\exists x)Fx$ but not $(\exists x)KFx$, a situation already contemplated in chapter 1.

8. A uniquely characterizing description on the order of "the tallest person in the room" will single out a particular individual without specifically identifying him.

9. The classic Paradox of the Heap (Sorites) affords an illustration. We know abstractly there is *some* number n as of which collected sand grains come to constitute a heap, but there is no *specifiable* number n of which we can say that this begins to be so.

10. To be sure, one could (truthfully) say something like, "The individual who prepared Caesar's breakfast on the fatal Ides of March is now totally unknown." But the person at issue here goes altogether unknown; that is, he or she is alluded to but not specified—individuated but not concretely identified. So I cannot appropriately claim to know *who* the individual at issue is but only at best *that* a certain individual is at issue.

11. On cognitive blindspots, see Roy A. Sorenson, *Blindspots* (Oxford: Clarendon Press, 1988).

12. See Paul Vincent Spade, "Insolubilia," in *The Cambridge History of Later Medieval Philosophy*, ed. Norman Kretzmann, Anthony Kenny, and Jan Pinborg (Cambridge: Cambridge University Press, 1982), 246–53.

13. Nor will we be concerned here with the issue of indemonstrable truths and unanswerable questions in mathematics. Our concern is only with *factual* truths, and the issue of truth in such formal descriptions as mathematics or logic will be left aside.

14. On this basis, Q is a globally intractable question iff:

$$(\exists p)(p @ Q \, \& \sim(\exists p)(\exists x)\Diamond Kx[p @ Q])$$

where $p @ Q$ iff the proposition p gives a (correct) answer to the question Q.

15. This issue here is one of so-called vagrant predicates that have no known address.

16. Charles S. Pierre, *Collected Papers of Charles Sanders Pierre* (Cambridge, Mass: Harvard University Press, 1931–58), 6:6.556.

17. And of course there are many other plausible theses of this sort; for example, "As long as scientific inquiry continues in the universe, every scientific discovery will eventually be improved upon and refined."

18. On the issues of this chapter, see also the author's *Epistemic Logic* (Pittsburgh: University of Pittsburgh Press, 2005).

CHAPTER 3. COGNITIVE SHORTFALL

1. For details, see the author's "Coordinating Epistemology and Ontology in Leibniz," in his *Studies on Leibniz's Cosmology* (Frankfurt: Ontos, 2006), 171–99.

2. Compare Philip Hugly and Charles Sayward, "Can a Language Have Indenumerably Many Expressions?" *History and Philosophy of Logic* 4 (1983): 73–82.

3. This supposes an upper limit to the length of intelligible statements. And even if this restriction were waived, the number of statements will still be no more than *countably* infinite.

4. Our position thus takes no issue with P. F. Strawson's precept that "facts are what statements (when true) state" ("Truth," *Proceedings of the Aristotelian Society* 24 [1950]: 129–56; see p. 136). Difficulty would ensue with Strawson's thesis only if an "only" were added.

5. To deny inferentially implicit information, the title of authentic *novelty* is not, of course, to say that it cannot *surprise* us in view of the limitations of our own deductive powers.

6. This also explains why the dispute over mathematical realism (Platonism) has little bearing on the issue of physical realism. Mathematical entities are akin to fictional entities in this—that we can only say about them what we can extract by deductive means from what we have ex-

plicitly put into their defining characterization. These abstract entities do not have nongeneric properties, since each is a "lowest species" unto itself.

7. Even in matters of actual linguistic practice we find an embarrassing shortcoming of words. The difficulty in adapting a compact vocabulary to the complexities of a diversified world are betokened by the pervasive phenomenon of polysemy—the contextualized pluralism of varied senses and differentiated uses of the same words in different semantical and grammatical categories. On this phenomenon, see Hubert Cuyckens and Britta Zawada, eds., *Polysemy in Cognitive Linguistics* (Amsterdam: John Benjamins, 2003).

8. We here take "counting" to be a matter of indicating integers by name—for example, as "thirteen" or "13"—rather than descriptively, as per "the first prime after eleven."

9. Wittgenstein writes, "logic is not a body of doctrine, but a mirror-image of the world" (*Tractatus*, 6.13). This surely gets it wrong: Logic is one instrumentality (among others) for organizing our thought about the world, and this thought is (as best and at most) a venture in *describing* or *conceiving* the world and its modus operandi in a way that—life being what it is—will inevitably be imperfect and incomplete. And so any talk of mirroring is a totally unrealistic exaggeration here.

10. Some of the issues of this chapter are also treated in the author's *Epistemetrics* (Cambridge: Cambridge University Press, 2005).

CHAPTER 4. COGNITIVE FINITUDE

1. To be sure, the prospect of inductively secured knowledge of laws is a philosophically controversial issue. But this is not the place to pursue it. (For the author's position, see his *Induction* [Oxford: Blackwell, 1980].)

2. The mathematical counterpart to such surdity is *randomness*. Thus a series on the order of 010011 . . . is random when there is no specifiable law to characterize its composition.

3. St. Thomas Aquinas, "Questions on God," in *Summa Theologica*, Q.12, §12.

CHAPTER 5. ON LIMITS TO SCIENCE

1. Lewis Thomas, as quoted in John Barthell, *Familiar Quotations*, 15th ed. (Boston & Toronto: Little Brown, 1980), 884, item 5.

2. Karl Pearson, *The Grammar of Science* (London: A. and C. Black, 1892), 22.

3. Note that this is independent of the question "Would we ever want to do so?" Do we ever want to answer all those predictive questions about ourselves and our environment, or are we more comfortable in the condition in which "ignorance is bliss"?

4. Of course these questions already exist. What lies in the future is not their existence but their presence on the agenda of active concern.

5. One possible misunderstanding must be blocked at this point. To learn about nature, we must interact with it. And so, to determine some feature of an object, we may have to make some impact upon it that would perturb its otherwise obtaining condition. (That indeterminacy principle of quantum theory affords a well-known reminder of this.) It should be clear that this matter of physical interaction for data acquisition is not contested in the ontological indifference thesis at issue here.

6. S. W. Hawking, "Is the End in Sight for Theoretical Physics?" *Physics Bulletin* 32 (1981): 15–17.

7. As stated, this question involves a bit of anthropomorphism in its use of "you." But this is so only for reasons of stylistic vivacity. That "you" could, of course, stand in for "computer number such-and-such."

8. Recall the anecdote of the musician who answered the question, "Where is jazz heading?" with the response, "If I knew that, I'd be there already."

9. For further detail on these issues, see the author's *The Limits of Science* (Pittsburgh: University of Pittsburgh Press, 1999).

10. On this theme, see the author's *Kant and the Reach of Reason: Stud-*

ies in Kant's Theory of Rational Systematization (Cambridge: Cambridge University Press, 2000).

11. This sentiment was abroad among physicists of the fin de siècle era of 1890–1900, and such sentiments are coming back into fashion today (Lawrence Badash, "The Completeness of Nineteenth-Century Science," *Isis* 63 [1972]: 48–58). See Richard Feynman, *The Character of Physical Law* (Cambridge, Mass.: MIT Press, 1965), 172; Gunther Stent, *The Coming of the Golden Age* (Garden City, N.Y.: Natural History Press, 1969); and S. W. Hawkins, "Is the End in Sight for Theoretical Physics?" *Physics Bulletin* 32 (1981): 15–17.

12. See Eber Jeffrey, "Nothing Left to Invent," *Journal of the Patent Office Society* 22 (July 1940): 479–81.

13. This inference could only be made if we could move from a thesis of the format $\sim(\exists r)(r \in S \; \& \; r \Rightarrow p)$ to one of the format $(\exists r)(r \in S \; \& \; r \Rightarrow \sim p)$, where "$\Rightarrow$" represents a grounding relationship of "furnishing a good reason," and p is, in this case, the particular thesis "S will at some point require drastic revision." That is, the inference would go through only if the lack (in S) of a good reason for p were itself to assure the existence (in S) of a good reason for $\sim p$. But the transition to this conclusion from the given premise would go through only if the former, antecedent fact itself constituted such a good reason—that is, only if we have $\sim(\exists r)(r \in S \; \& \; r \Rightarrow p) \Rightarrow \sim p$. Thus, the inference would go through only if, by the contraposition, $p \Rightarrow (\exists r)(r \in S \; \& \; r \Rightarrow p)$. This thesis claims that the very truth of p will itself be a good reason to hold that S affords a good reason for p—in sum, that S is complete.

14. See the author's *Peirce's Philosophy of Science* (Notre Dame: University of Notre Dame Press, 1978).

15. Some further aspects of this chapter's themes are presented in the author's *The Limits of Science*.

CHAPTER 6. OBSTACLES TO PREDICTIVE FOREKNOWLEDGE

1. On these issues, see also the author's *Predicting the Future* (Albany: State University of New York Press, 1997).

CHAPTER 7. CAN COMPUTERS MEND MATTERS?

1. The salient point is that unless I can *determine* (i.e., myself be able to claim justifiably) that you are warranted in offering your response, I have no adequate grounds to accept it as answering my question: it has not been made credible to me, irrespective of how justified you may be in regard to it. To be sure, for your claim to be credible for me, I need not know *what* your justification for it is, but I must be in a position to realize *that* you are justified. Your reasons may even be incomprehensible to me, but for credibility I require a rationally warranted assurance— perhaps only on the basis of general principles—that those reasons are both extant and cogent.

2. On unsolvable calculating problems, mathematical completeness, and computability, see Martin Davis, *Computability and Unsolvability* (New York: McGraw-Hill, 1958; expanded reprint ed., New York: Dover, 1982). See also N. B. Pour-El and J. I. Richards, *Computability in Analysis and Physics* (Berlin: Springer Verlag, 1989), or on a more popular level, Douglas Hofstadter, *Gödel, Escher, Bach: An Eternal Golden Braid* (New York: Basic Books, 1979).

3. Some problems are not inherently unsolvable, but they cannot in principle be settled by computers; for instance, "What is an example of a word that no computer will ever use?" Such problems are inherently computer-inappropriate and for this reason a failure to handle them satisfactorily also cannot be seen as a meaningful limitation of computers.

4. On Gödel's theorem, see S. G. Shanker, ed., *Gödel's Theorems in Focus* (London: Croom Helm, 1988), a collection of essays that provide instructive, personal, philosophical, and mathematical perspectives on Gödel's work.

5. For a comprehensive survey of the physical limitations of computers, see Theodore Leiber, "Chaos, Berechnungskomplexität und Physik: Neue Grenzen wissenschaftlicher Erkenntnis," *Philosophia Naturalis* 34 (1997): 23–54.

6. Here again, "you" is only shorthand for "computer number such-and-such."

7. On the inherent limitation of predictions, see the author's *Predicting the Future*.

8. Cambridge, Mass.: MIT Press, 1992. This book is an updated version of his earlier *What Computers Can't Do* (New York: Harper Collins, 1972).

9. For some discussion of this issue from a very different point of approach, see Roger Penrose, *The Emperor's New Mind* (New York: Oxford University Press, 1989).

10. We have just claimed P_5 as computer irresolvable. And this contention, of course, entails $(\exists P)(\forall C)\sim C$ res P or equivalently $\sim(\forall P)(\exists C)C$ res P. Letting this thesis be T_3, we may recall that T_2 comes to $(\forall C)\sim C$ det $\sim T_3$. If T_3 is indeed true, then this contention—that is, T_2—will of course immediately follow.

11. Someone might suggest, "But one can use the same line of thought to show that there are computer-solvable problems that people cannot possibly solve by simply interchanging the reference to 'computers' and 'people' throughout its preceding argumentation." But this will not do. For the fact that it is people that use computers means that one can credit people with computer-provided problem solutions via the idea that *people can solve problems with computers*. But the reverse cannot be claimed with any semblance of plausibility. The situation is not in fact symmetrical, and so the proposed interchange will not work. This issue will be elaborated in the next section.

12. On the issues of this chapter, see also the author's *The Limits of Science*.

CHAPTER 8. IMPLICATIONS OF IGNORANCE

1. Examples of this sort indicate why philosophers are unwilling to identify *knowledge* with *true belief*.

2. This circumstance did not elude Neils Bohr himself, the father of complementarity theory in physics: "In later years Bohr emphasized the importance of complementarity for matters far removed from physics. There is a story that Bohr was once asked in German what is the qual-

ity that is complementary to truth (*Wahrheit*). After some thought he answered clarity (*Klarheit*)" (Stephen Weinberg, *Dreams of a Final Theory* [New York: Pantheon Books, 1992], 74 n10.)

3. The present deliberations have a deep kinship with the doctrines of Nicholas of Cusa. His classic *De docta ignorantia* pioneered the idea that knowledge can—and to some extent must—take root in ignorance. And his doctrine of "coincidence of opposites" also comes into the picture. However, "coincidence" must not be understood here as total agreement (sameness) but as the sense of coming together, of being in contact or touch. It is not the same thing to travel clockwise or counterclockwise in a circle, but eventually you will reach the same point. Knowledge and ignorance are different things, but in many cases one of them can be achieved through the mediation of its opposite.

4. On these issues, see also the author's *Complexity* (New Brunswick, N.J.: Transaction Publishers, 1998).

BIBLIOGRAPHY

Badash, Lawrence. "The Completeness of Nineteenth-Century Science." *Isis* 63 (1972): 48–58.

Cairns, John. *An Examination of Professor Ferrier's "Theory of Knowing and Being."* Edinburgh: Thos. Constable & Co., 1856.

Davis, Martin. *Computability and Unsolvability.* New York: McGraw-Hill, 1958; expanded reprint ed., New York: Dover, 1982.

Ferrier, James F. *Institutes of Metaphysics.* Bristol: Thoemones Press, 2001.

———. *The Philosophical Works of the Late James Frederick Ferrier.* 3 vols. Edinburgh: W. Blackwood and Sons, 1875–88.

Feynman, Richard. *The Character of Physical Law.* Cambridge, Mass.: MIT Press, 1965.

Hawking, S. W. "Is the End in Sight for Theoretical Physics?" *Physics Bulletin* 32 (1981): 15–17.

Hofstadter, Douglas. *Gödel, Escher, Bach: An Eternal Golden Braid.* New York: Basic Books, 1979.

Hugly, Philip, and Charles Sayward. "Can a Language Have Indenumerably Many Expressions?" *History and Philosophy of Logic* 4 (1983): 73–82.

Jeffrey, Eber. "Nothing Left to Invent." *Journal of the Patent Office Society* 22 (July 1940): 479–81.

Kant, Immanuel. *Critique of Pure Reason.* 1781.

———. *Prolegomena to Any Future Metaphysic.* 1783.

Keefe, Jenny. "James Ferrier and the Theory of Ignorance." *Monist* 90 (2007): 297–309.

Leiber, Theodore. "Chaos, Berechnungskomplexität und Physik: Neue Grenzen wissenschaftlicher Erkenntnis." *Philosophia Naturalis* 34 (1997): 23–54.

Mach, Ernst. *Erkenntnis und Irrtum.* Leipzig: J. A. Barth, 1906.

Nicholas of Cusa. *De docta ignorantia.*

Pearson, Karl. *The Grammar of Science.* London: A. and C. Black, 1892.

Penrose, Roger. *The Emperor's New Mind.* New York: Oxford University Press, 1989.

Plato. *Apology.* Trans. Rev. Joseph Mills. Cambridge, England: J. Archdeacon, 1775.

Pour-El, N. B., and J. I. Richards. *Computability in Analysis and Physics.* Berlin: Springer Verlag, 1989.

Rescher, Nicholas. *Complexity.* New Brunswick, N.J.: Transaction Publishers, 1998.

———. "Coordinating Epistemology and Ontology in Leibniz." In Nicholas Rescher, *Studies on Leibniz's Cosmology,* 171–99. Frankfurt: Ontos, 2006.

———. *Epistemetrics.* Cambridge: Cambridge University Press, 2005.

———. *Epistemic Logic.* Pittsburgh: University of Pittsburgh Press, 2004.

———. *Induction.* Oxford: Blackwell, 1980.

———. *Kant and the Reach of Reason: Studies in Kant's Theory of Rational Systematization.* Cambridge: Cambridge University Press, 2000.

———. *The Limits of Science.* Berkeley: University of California Press, 1984; rev. ed., Pittsburgh: University of Pittsburgh Press, 1999.

———. *Peirce's Philosophy of Science.* Notre Dame: University of Notre Dame Press, 1978.

———. *Predicting the Future.* Albany: State University of New York Press, 1997.

———. *Scepticism: A Critical Reappraisal.* Oxford: Basil Blackwell, 1980.

Shanker, S. G., ed. *Gödel's Theorems in Focus.* London: Croom Helm, 1988.

Spade, Paul Vincent. "Insolubilia." In *The Cambridge History of Later Medieval Philosophy,* ed. Norman Kretzmann, Anthony Kenny, and Jan Pinborg, 246–53. Cambridge: Cambridge University Press, 1982.

Stent, Gunther. *The Coming of the Golden Age.* Garden City, N.Y.: Natural History Press, 1969.

Weinberg, Stephen. *Dreams of a Final Theory.* New York: Pantheon Books, 1992.

INDEX OF NAMES